UNE SAISON EN ENFER & LE BATEAU IVRE

A SEASON IN HELL & THE DRUNKEN BOAT

ENGLISH TRANSLATION BY LOUISE VARÈSE

A NEW DIRECTIONS PAPERBOOK

Library of Congress Catalog Card Number: 61-14900
ISBN: 0-8112-0185-6

First published as New Directions Paperbook No. 97 in 1961

Manufactured in the United States of America
New Directions books are printed on acid-free paper
Published in Canada by Penguin Books Canada Limited
New Directions Books are published for James Laughlin
by New Directions Publishing Corporation,
80 Eighth Avenue, New York 10011.

TWENTY-FOURTH PRINTING

A SEASON IN HELL

CONTENTS

A RIMBAUD CHRONOLOGY

Note: This chronology has been prepared by Hubert Creekmore for the Publisher. Its factual data is taken largely from the definitive biography of Rimbaud by Professor Enid Starkie, published in England by Faber & Faber, and in the United States by W. W. Norton.

October 20, 1854
Jean-Nicolas-Arthur Rimbaud was born at Charleville, a small French town on the Meuse near the borders of Belgium. He was the second son of a Captain Rimbaud, a Bourguignon, who had made a good record in the colonial administration of Algeria and, coming to Mézières with his regiment in 1852, married, apparently for her dowry, Vitalie Cuif, the daughter of a prosperous farmer of Roche, near Charleville. They had two boys and three girls (the oldest

girl dying in infancy) but the marriage was not a success; and when Arthur Rimbaud was six, his father deserted his mother and never returned home. The character of Madame Rimbaud would seem to be a sufficient excuse for his desertion. She was a bigoted, hard, stubborn, arrogant woman with an iron will, who probably made as little effort to understand her husband as later to understand her genius son. Rimbaud has written a merciless indictment of her in his poem *Les Poètes de Sept Ans.*

1860–1870

With only a small income to support her family, Madame Rimbaud moved to a slum-like section of Charleville where for two years she lived in proud seclusion among the poor. But the sympathy of her son Arthur was excited by the poverty around him, and he spent secretly many hours with the neighborhood children. When his mother learned of his adventures, she began to fear that her boys would acquire the coarse manners of workmen, and by some means she contrived to move to one of the best quarters of the town. Arthur, now eight, having been taught hitherto by his mother, began formal schooling at the Pension Rossat where his first literary work was composed. Madame Rimbaud, in her ambition for her sons, was ruthless in her supervision of their studies

and rarely allowed herself to display any affection for them. Forbidden the company of other boys and receiving no love from his mother, Arthur turned within himself and to reading in search of an intense life. Upon entering the Collège de Charleville, he soon attracted notice by his remarkable ability. His mother, foreseeing in him a brilliant scholar, loosened her tight purse strings to engage a private tutor, who stimulated in him a love of Greek, Latin and French literature and encouraged him in his gift for writing both Latin and French verses. Arthur's interests were gradually extended to modern literature, and under the influence of the dominant Parnassian school of poetry he wrote and published a poem in *La Revue pour Tous,* January, 1870.

1870

A twenty-one-year-old teacher, George Izambard, joined the staff of the Collège de Charleville and became the first great influence in Rimbaud's career. Izambard gave him the feeling of being understood that he had never before experienced. Arthur's reading spread over a wider range, but his mother protested this "dangerous" literature. Nevertheless, the friendship continued, with Arthur reading in his teacher's rooms and producing a number of derivative poems. At the close of school, he took first prize in the Con-

cours Académique and won many other prizes in examinations. Soon after this the Franco-Prussian War broke out and Izambard left Charleville. Arthur was despondent and talked of running away. At length he did so, but arriving in Paris with no money for his ticket, was arrested, imprisoned for a week and after writing for help to Izambard, was sent to him at Douai where he stayed for three weeks because of the disrupted communication system during war. On his return to Charleville, Madame Rimbaud, full of righteous anger and terrified by the trend toward unruly independence in her formerly obedient son, became more stupidly intolerant than ever, and Arthur ran away again almost at once. At his mother's plea, Izambard trailed him through several towns across the Belgian frontier before discovering him back at Douai copying new poems written on his wanderings. In Charleville once more, Arthur continued to "adore free freedom with horrible obstinacy," and to loathe his jailor. War prevented the reopening of the Collège and in his idleness he took endless walks with his friend Delahaye and read everything he could lay hands on including the work of the new poet Paul Verlaine. The Prussians later occupied Charleville, but soon an armistice was signed and the National Guard, amid the popular displeasure at the peace, planned a revolt. Arthur determined to join the uprising in Paris, sold

his watch for train fare and spent two weeks in the city, living on the streets and eating what he could find. In the midst of the excitement of the formation of the Commune, he suddenly returned to Charleville, a totally changed young man, embittered by experiences whose nature can only be surmised. Out of these came his first poem of deep feeling, *Coeur Supplicié,* and out of Izambard's unsympathetic reaction to the poem, the end of the friendship between them. From this time on, Rimbaud lived in a more or less complete state of alienation from conventional patterns of behavior. His revolt found expression in a life of filth, announced, even if unpractised, depravity and sullen denunciations of woman and church. Concurrently with the increase of this inner turmoil, he was reading occult and "immoral" literature and experiencing the revelation of Baudelaire's *Fleurs du Mal* which had been published in 1857. Rimbaud's rebellion against the bigoted, false, pretentious bourgeois life he knew burst in obscenities and blasphemies in his poetry of this period, but at the same time he was formulating the theories of poetry that were to shape his later work and to some extent his life. An iconoclastic customs official, Charles Bretagne, supplanted Izambard as a personal influence and encouraged him in Oriental and cabalistic philosophies which converged in his doctrine of the *voyant,* the theory that a poet must be a

visionary or seer. Bretagne, who knew Verlaine, suggested that Rimbaud write to him and himself added an introduction. In the letter Rimbaud enclosed some of his poems and received an enthusiastic reply from Verlaine and an invitation to come to Paris.

1871

Rimbaud's visit to the Verlaine household in Paris scandalized both the conservative family and the neighbors. His wife's parents felt that Verlaine, although twenty years older than Rimbaud, was being debauched by the young man; and eventually Rimbaud took lodgings elsewhere. He had no money, but Verlaine secured for him an attic in the house of Théodore de Banville and a subscription from several friends to meet expenses. Rimbaud's life in Paris was disorderly and unstable; he lived uncleanly, took drugs and moved from one friend's hospitality to another's. He antagonized all the literary men he met by his scathing criticism and arrogance. In the end only Verlaine remained tolerant, renting him a room and carousing with him there and in cafés to the disgust of Verlaine's circle of conservative literary men. Early in 1872, in the complete emotional, intellectual and spiritual fulfilment of his relationship with Verlaine, Rimbaud began to write some of the prose poems and verses later entitled *Les Illuminations*. The conduct of

the two poets became too scandalous to hide, and Mme. Verlaine, after much mental and physical suffering (some of which, to be sure, had preceded Rimbaud's arrival) threatened to leave her husband unless Rimbaud were sent back to Charleville. Verlaine gave in and Rimbaud went home; but it was not long before Verlaine sent for him and they set off on a trip to Brussels. Mme. Verlaine followed them there and persuaded her husband to return with her, but he deserted again at the frontier, rejoined Rimbaud and after two months in Belgium they crossed to England.

September, 1872

In London, Rimbaud and Verlaine found quarters in the bohemian Soho district where many French exiles of the Commune were living. They gave lessons in French when they could find such work, and may possibly have met some of the rising young English poets. In France, Mme. Verlaine was now taking steps to secure a legal separation and had so informed Rimbaud's mother. Mme. Rimbaud summoned her son home from London, hoping to keep his name out of the case. But the following January, Verlaine, ill with influenza, recalled Rimbaud by picturing himself as dying alone in a strange city; and their debauchery was resumed. During this period, Rimbaud felt a growing disgust for Verlaine's sentimentality and

wished to separate himself from what he now considered a debilitating influence. In April, 1873, the two men returned separately to France, and Rimbaud went to his family farm at Roche where he began writing *Une Saison en Enfer.* Within a month, however, Verlaine had persuaded him to go back to England; but the happiness of their association was gone and they eventually quarreled. Verlaine sailed to Belgium and wrote his mother that he intended to kill himself. Later he wired Rimbaud to join him in Brussels. Rimbaud found him drunk and displaying all the weakness of character which now so repelled him. When he announced that he was leaving, Verlaine shot at him three times with a revolver, striking him once in the wrist. Mme. Verlaine and Rimbaud managed to quiet his hysteria, but when, on the way to the railroad station, Rimbaud remained firm in his decision to leave, Verlaine again lost control and threatened him. Rimbaud called for police protection. Verlaine was arrested, tried and sentenced to two years' hard labor and a fine. Rimbaud went home and in a fever of work and suffering finished *Une Saison en Enfer*. He had it printed soon afterward and sent copies to literary friends in Paris, where he himself followed to see how it was received. Because of the Brussels scandal, he found himself snubbed, personally and artistically,

and returned to Charleville to burn all his manuscripts, letters and his remaining author's copies of *Une Saison en Enfer*. At the age of nineteen, he ended his literary career and probably never wrote poetry again.

1873–1879

Disillusioned with literature and still bent on getting away from home, Rimbaud took up the study of languages and began a period of wandering over Europe. He went first to Paris and then, in company with Germain Nouveau, a poet a year or two older than himself, to London. In 1875 he traveled to Germany, and in Stuttgart, Verlaine, just released and full of his new religious zeal acquired in prison, joined him. Of this visit which lasted two and a half days, Rimbaud wrote in a letter to his old friend Delahaye: "Verlaine arrived here the other day pawing a rosary. . . Three hours later he had denied his God and started the 98 wounds of Our Lord bleeding again." Rimbaud went next to Italy, crossing the Alps on foot. Headed for Paros where he hoped to work in a soap factory, he suffered a sunstroke, was sent to Marseilles, finally reached Paris and went on to Charleville. December found him again in London for a short time, and then he was on his way to Russia. But he was robbed in Vienna and returned through Germany to France. At

various times he thought of completing his baccalaureate so that he could teach in the college and oddly enough, of learning to play the piano. At last he went to Holland where, in order to reach the Orient, he enlisted in the Dutch army and sailed for Java in June of 1876. Three weeks after his arrival in Batavia he deserted, wandered among the natives of the jungle and soon signed on a British ship for Liverpool. After a winter at home he went to Hamburg, joined a circus as interpreter-manager to tour the northern countries, but the cold was too much for him and he was repatriated from Sweden, only to leave home again, this time for Alexandria. Again illness interrupted his travels and he was put off the ship in Italy and spent a year recovering on the farm at Roche. In 1878 he was in Hamburg again, trying to reach Genoa to take a ship for the East. Once more he tried to cross the Alps on foot, but in a snowstorm he almost perished. Saved by monks in a Hospice, he managed to reach Genoa and sail to Alexandria where he worked as a farm laborer for a while. In Suez, where he stopped on his way to Cyprus, he was employed as ship-breaker to plunder a ship wrecked on the dangerous coast at Guardafui. Most of the first half of 1879 he worked as foreman in a desert quarry on Cyprus, and went home in June to recuperate from typhoid fever.

1880–1890
None of his friends ever saw Rimbaud again after he left for Cyprus in 1880 to manage a gang of construction workers. Later he sailed down the Red Sea, took fever in Aden and was sheltered and given work by a French trader named Bardey. In November, 1880, Rimbaud set out for Harar in Abyssinia to manage a trading post for Bardey. As the first European to reside in Harar, he wished to write a report on the country and to explore further. In 1884 his account of a trip into unknown regions, sponsored by Bardey in the interest of an expanding market, was printed by the Société de Géographie. Rimbaud was ill with syphilis, suffered deeply from loneliness and inactivity, but at the same time never bothered to concern himself with the outside world. When he did not answer a letter from Verlaine, the older poet assumed that he was dead and had an edition of his poems published in 1886. Following conflicts between Egypt and Abyssinia, Harar reverted to its former Moslem rulers, and the European traders fled. Rimbaud went back to Aden taking with him a girl of the Harari tribe who lived with him for about a year. The juggling for power on the Red Sea between European and Eastern Sudanese rulers had reached a stage which made traffic in firearms with King Menelek of Shoa a profitable enter-

prise. Rimbaud quarreled with Bardey and decided to make his fortune in gun-running to the interior. By October, 1886, after many months of waiting and preparation, he started his caravan on the dangerous journey from Tajoura to Ankober, arriving there in February, 1887. Menelek, taking advantage of Rimbaud's inexperience, fleeced him with clever financial complications and when Rimbaud finally returned to the coast he had lost all his resources. He published an account of his trip in a journal in Cairo, applied vainly to *Le Temps* as war correspondent for the first Italian-Abyssinian War and at last in May, 1888 returned to Harar as partner of two established gun-runners and slave-traders. His main interest was now to make a fortune that would leave him independent, but it was slow to accumulate. Although he had frequent explorer visitors, we know from his letters home asking for scientific books and instruments that he wanted a fuller intellectual life. Apparently his only source of happiness was his servant and companion, Djami. After all the "fatigues, adventures and nameless hardships" he seems to have begun to long for repose and even toyed with the idea of returning to France to find a wife. As he wrote in a letter to his mother, he wanted "at least to have a son whom I could spend my life bringing up according to my ideas, arming him with the most complete education to be had today

and who would become a renowned engineer, a man made rich and powerful through science."

1891

By the time he left Harar on April 2, 1891, Rimbaud was suffering from a swelling of his right leg where an inflammation had been steadily increasing for some months. When a stay in the hospital at Aden brought no relief, he said goodbye to Djami and went on to France. In a Marseilles hospital his right leg was amputated. In July he reached the farm at Roche after an absence of twelve years. His sister Isabelle now gave him the attention and affection that had been lacking in his early family life ("women nurse those fierce invalids home from hot countries"); but a month in the bleak farmhouse convinced Rimbaud that he must seek the warm sun of the East. Disease had spread further through his body when he started for Marseilles accompanied by Isabelle. In the hospital there she watched over him tenderly and rejoiced at his feverish death-bed return to the Church against which he had so long rebelled. He became paralysed. The doctors diagnosed the disease as carcinoma, but it may have been syphilis in the tertiary stage. In his delirium, Rimbaud thought always of Harar. Before he died on November 10, 1891, he asked that a legacy of three thousand francs be sent to his servant Djami in Harar.

He was buried in Charleville and ten years later a monument was erected to his memory in the Square de la Gare.

UNE SAISON EN ENFER

UNE SAISON EN ENFER

JADIS, si je me souviens bien, ma vie était un festin où s'ouvraient tous les cœurs, où tous les vins coulaient.

Un soir, j'ai assis la Beauté sur mes genoux.—Et je l'ai trouvée amère.—Et je l'ai injuriée.

Je me suis armé contre la justice.

Je me suis enfui. O sorcières, ô misère, ô haine, c'est à vous que mon trésor a été confié!

Je parvins à faire s'évanouir dans mon esprit toute l'espérance humaine. Sur toute joie, pour l'étrangler, j'ai fait le bond sourd de la bête féroce.

J'ai appelé les bourreaux pour, en périssant, mordre la crosse de leurs fusils. J'ai appelé les fléaux, pour m'étouffer avec le sable, le sang. Le malheur a été mon dieu. Je me suis allongé dans la boue. Je me suis séché à l'air du crime. Et j'ai joué de bons tours à la folie.

A SEASON IN HELL

ONCE, if I remember well, my life was a feast where all hearts opened and all wines flowed.

One evening I seated Beauty on my knees. And I found her bitter. And I cursed her.

I armed myself against justice.

I fled. O Witches, O Misery, O Hate, to you has my treasure been entrusted!

I contrived to purge my mind of all human hope. On all joy, to strangle it, I pounced with the stealth of a wild beast.

I called to the executioners that I might gnaw their rifle-butts while dying. I called to the plagues to smother me in blood, in sand. Misfortune was my God. I laid myself down in the mud. I dried myself in the air of crime. I played sly tricks on madness.

Et le printemps m'a apporté l'affreux rire de l'idiot.

Or, tout dernièrement, m'étant trouvé sur le point de faire le dernier *couac,* j'ai songé à rechercher la clef du festin ancien, où je reprendrais peut-être appétit.

La charité est cette clef.—Cette inspiration prouve que j'ai rêvé!

"Tu resteras hyène. . ." etc., se récrie le démon qui me couronna de si aimables pavots. "Gagne la mort avec tous tes appétits, et ton égoïsme et tous les péchés capitaux."

Ah! j'en ai trop pris:—Mais, cher Satan, je vous en conjure, une prunelle moins irritée! et en attendant les quelques petites lâchetés en retard, vous qui aimez dans l'écrivain l'absence des facultés descriptives ou instructives, je vous détache ces quelques hideux feuillets de mon carnet de damné.

And spring brought me the idiot's frightful laughter.

Now, only recently, being on the point of giving my last squawk, I thought of looking for the key to the ancient feast where I might find my appetite again.

Charity is that key.—This inspiration proves that I have dreamed!

"You will always be a hyena. . ." etc., protests the devil who crowned me with such pleasant poppies. "Attain death with all your appetites, your selfishness and all the capital sins!"

Ah! I'm fed up:—But, dear Satan, a less fiery eye I beg you! And while awaiting a few small infamies in arrears, you who love the absence of the instructive or descriptive faculty in a writer, for you let me tear out these few, hideous pages from my notebook of one of the damned.

MAUVAIS SANG

J'ai de mes ancêtres gaulois l'œil bleu blanc, la cervelle étroite, et la maladresse dans la lutte. Je trouve mon habillement aussi barbare que le leur. Mais je ne beurre pas ma chevelure.

Les Gaulois étaient les écorcheurs de bêtes, les brûleurs d'herbes les plus ineptes de leur temps.

D'eux, j'ai: l'idolâtrie et l'amour du sacrilège;—oh! tous les vices, colère, luxure,—magnifique, la luxure;—surtout mensonge et paresse.

J'ai horreur de tous les métiers. Maîtres et ouvriers, tous paysans, ignobles. La main à plume vaut la main à charrue.—Quel siècle à mains!—Je n'aurai jamais ma main. Après, la domesticité mène trop loin. L'honnêteté de la mendicité me navre. Les criminels dégoûtent comme des châtrés: moi, je suis intact, et ça m'est égal.

BAD BLOOD

I have the white-blue eye of my Gallic ancestors, their narrow skull and their clumsiness in fighting. I find my clothes as barbarous as theirs. Only I don't butter my hair.

The Gauls were the most inept flayers of beasts and scorchers of grass of their time.

From them too: idolatry and love of sacrilege; oh! all the vices, anger, lust—lust, magnificent—above all, lying and sloth.

I have a horror of all trades. Masters and workers —base peasants all. The hand that guides the pen is worth the hand that guides the plough.—What an age of hands! I shall never have my hand. Afterward domesticity leads too far. The honesty of beggars sickens me. Criminals disgust like castrates: as for me, I am intact, and I don't care.

Mais! qui a fait ma langue perfide tellement, qu'elle ait guidé et sauvegardé jusqu'ici ma paresse? Sans me servir pour vivre même de mon corps, et plus oisif que le crapaud, j'ai vécu partout. Pas une famille d'Europe que je ne connaisse.—J'entends des familles comme la mienne, qui tiennent tout de la déclaration des Droits de l'Homme.—J'ai connu chaque fils de famille!

* * *

Si j'avais des antécédents à un point quelconque de l'histoire de France!

Mais non, rien.

Il m'est bien évident que j'ai toujours été race inférieure. Je ne puis comprendre la révolte. Ma race ne se souleva jamais que pour piller: tels les loups à la bête qu'ils n'ont pas tuée.

Je me rappelle l'histoire de la France, fille aînée de l'Eglise. J'aurais fait, manant, le voyage de terre sainte; j'ai dans la tête des routes dans les plaines souabes, des vues de Byzance, des remparts de Solyme: le culte de Marie, l'attendrissement sur le Crucifié s'éveillent en moi parmi mille féeries profanes.—Je suis assis, lépreux, sur les pots cassés et les orties, au pied d'un mur rongé par le soleil.—Plus tard, reître, j'aurais bivaqué sous les nuits d'Allemagne.

But who gave me so perfidious a tongue that it has guided and guarded my indolence till now? Without even using my body for a living, and lazier than the toad, I have lived everywhere. Not a family of Europe that I do not know.—I mean families like my own that owe everything to the Declaration of the Rights of Man.—I have known all the sons of good families.

* * *

Had I but antecedents at some point in the history of France!

But no, nothing.

It is quite clear to me that I have always been of an inferior race. I cannot understand revolt. My race never rose except to pillage: like wolves that worry the beast they have not killed.

I recall the history of France, eldest daughter of the Church. A villein, I must have made the journey to the Holy Land; my head is full of roads through the Swabian plains, views of Byzantium, ramparts of Jerusalem: The cult of Mary, compassion for the crucified Christ awake in me among a thousand profane phantasmagoria.—A leper, I am seated among potsherds and nettles, at the foot of a sun-eaten wall.—Later, a reiter, I must have bivouacked under German stars.

Ah! encore: je danse le sabbat dans une rouge clairière, avec des vieilles et des enfants.

Je ne me souviens pas plus loin que cette terre-ci et le christianisme. Je n'en finirais pas de me revoir dans ce passé. Mais toujours seul; sans famille; même, quelle langue parlais-je? Je ne me vois jamais dans les conseils du Christ; ni dans les conseils des Seigneurs, —représentants du Christ.

Qu'étais-je au siècle dernier: je ne me retrouve qu'aujourd'hui. Plus de vagabonds, plus de guerres vagues. La race inférieure a tout couvert—le peuple, comme on dit, la raison, la nation et la science.

Oh! la science! On a tout repris. Pour le corps et pour l'âme,—le viatique,—on a la médecine et la philosophie,—les remèdes de bonnes femmes et les chansons populaires arrangées. Et les divertissements des princes et les jeux qu'ils interdisaient! Géographie, cosmographie, mécanique, chimie! . . .

La science, la nouvelle noblesse! Le progrès. Le monde marche! Pourquoi ne tournerait-il pas?

C'est la vision des nombres. Nous allons à l'*Esprit*. C'est très certain, c'est oracle, ce que je dis. Je comprends, et ne sachant m'expliquer sans paroles païennes, je voudrais me taire.

* * *

Le sang païen revient! L'Esprit est proche; pourquoi Christ ne m'aide-t-il pas, en donnant à mon

Ah! what's more: I dance the witches' sabbath in a red clearing with old women and children.

I can remember no farther back than this very land and Christianity. I shall never have done seeing myself in that past. But always alone; without family; and even the language that I spoke—what was it? I cannot see myself at the councils of Christ; nor at the councils of Nobles—representatives of Christ.

What was I in the last century? I find no trace again until today. No more vagabonds, no more vague wars. The inferior race has over-run everything—the people, as we say, the nation, reason, science.

Oh! Science! Everything has been revised. For the body and for the soul,—the viaticum,—there are medicine and philosophy,—old wives' remedies and popular songs rearranged. And the pastimes of princes and games they proscribed! Geography, cosmography, mechanics, chemistry! . . .

Science, the new nobility! Progress. The world marches on! Why shouldn't it turn?

It is the vision of numbers. We are going toward the *Spirit*. There's no doubt about it, an oracle, I tell you. I understand, and not knowing how to express myself without pagan words, I'd rather remain silent.

* * *

Pagan blood returns! The Spirit is near; why doesn't Christ help me by granting my soul nobility

âme noblesse et liberté? Hélas, l'Evangile a passé! l'Evangile! l'Evangile.

J'attends Dieu avec gourmandise. Je suis de race inférieure de toute éternité.

Me voici sur la plage armoricaine. Que les villes s'allument dans le soir. Ma journée est faite; je quitte l'Europe. L'air marin brûlera mes poumons; les climats perdus me tanneront. Nager, broyer l'herbe, chasser, fumer surtout; boire des liqueurs fortes comme du métal bouillant,—comme faisaient ces chers ancêtres autour des feux.

Je reviendrai, avec des membres de fer, la peau sombre, l'œil furieux; sur mon masque, on me jugera d'une race forte. J'aurai de l'or: je serai oisif et brutal. Les femmes soignent ces féroces infirmes retour des pays chauds. Je serai mêlé aux affaires politiques. Sauvé.

Maintenant je suis maudit, j'ai horreur de la patrie. Le meilleur, c'est un sommeil bien ivre sur la grève.

* * *

On ne part pas.—Reprenons les chemins d'ici, chargé de mon vice, le vice qui a poussé ses racines de souffrance à mon côté, dès l'âge de raison,—qui monte au ciel, me bat, me renverse, me traîne.

La dernière innocence et la dernière timidité. C'est dit. Ne pas porter au monde mes dégoûts et mes trahisons.

and liberty? Alas! The Gospel has gone by! The Gospel! The Gospel.

Greedily I await God. I am of an inferior race for all eternity.

Here I am on the Breton shore. Let the towns light up in the evening. My day is done; I'm quitting Europe. Sea air will burn my lungs; strange climates will tan my skin. To swim, to trample the grass, to hunt, and above all to smoke; to drink liquors strong as boiling metal,—like my dear ancestors around their fires.

I'll return with limbs of iron, dark skin and furious eye; people will think to look at me that I am of a strong race. I will have gold: I will be idle and brutal. Women nurse those fierce invalids, home from hot countries. I'll be mixed up in politics. Saved.

Now I am an outcast. I loathe the fatherland. The thing for me is a very drunken sleep on the beach.

* * *

We're not going.—Back over the old roads again, laden with my vice, the vice whose roots of suffering have flourished at my side since reason dawned,—that rises to the skies, belabours me, knocks me down, drags me along.

The last innocence and the last timidity. It's settled. Not to display my betrayals and disgusts to the world.

Allons! La marche, le fardeau, le désert, l'ennui et la colère.

A qui me louer? Quelle bête faut-il adorer? Quelle sainte image attaque-t-on? Quels cœurs briserai-je? Quel mensonge dois-je tenir?—Dans quel sang marcher?

Plutôt, se garder de la justice.—La vie dure, l'abrutissement simple,—soulever, le poing desséché, le couvercle du cercueil, s'asseoir, s'étouffer. Ainsi point de vieillesse, ni de dangers: la terreur n'est pas française.

—Ah! je suis tellement délaissé que j'offre à n'importe quelle divine image des élans vers la perfection.

O mon abnégation, ô ma charité merveilleuse! ici-bas, pourtant!

De profundis, Domine, suis-je bête!

* * *

Encore tout enfant, j'admirais le forçat intraitable sur qui se referme toujours le bagne; je visitais les auberges et les garnis qu'il aurait sacrés par son séjour; je voyais *avec son idée* le ciel bleu et le travail fleuri de la campagne; je flairais sa fatalité dans les villes. Il avait plus de force qu'un saint, plus de bon sens qu'un voyageur,—et lui, lui seul! pour témoin de sa gloire et de sa raison.

Sur les routes, par des nuits d'hiver, sans gîte, sans habits, sans pain, une voix étreignait mon cœur gelé:

Forward! The march, the burden and the desert, weariness and anger.

To whom shall I hire myself out? What beast should I adore? What holy image is attacked? What hearts shall I break? What lies should I uphold? In what blood tread?

Rather steer clear of the law.—The hard life, simple brutishness,—to lift with withered fist the coffin's lid, to sit, to suffocate. And thus no old age, no dangers: terror is not French.

—Ah! I am so utterly forsaken that to any divine image whatsoever, I offer my impulses toward perfection.

O my abnegation, O my marvelous charity! here below, however!

De profundis, Domine, what a fool I am!

* * *

Still but a child, I admired the intractable convict on whom the prison doors are always closing; I sought out the inns and rooming houses he would have consecrated by his passing; *with his idea* I saw the blue sky, and the flowery labor of the country; in cities I sensed his fatality. He had more strength than a saint, more common sense than a traveler—and he, he alone! the witness of his glory and his reason.

On highroads on winter nights, without roof, without clothes, without bread, a voice gripped my frozen

"Faiblesse ou force: te voilà, c'est la force. Tu ne sais ni où tu vas, ni pourquoi tu vas; entre partout, réponds à tout. On ne te tuera pas plus que si tu étais cadavre." Au matin j'avais le regard si perdu et la contenance si morte, que ceux que j'ai rencontrés *ne m'ont peut-être pas vu.*

Dans les villes la boue m'apparaissait soudainement rouge et noire, comme une glace quand la lampe circule dans la chambre voisine, comme un trésor dans la forêt! Bonne chance, criai-je, et je voyais une mer de flammes et de fumée au ciel; et, à gauche, à droite, toutes les richesses flambant comme un milliard de tonnerres.

Mais l'orgie et la camaraderie des femmes m'étaient interdites. Pas même un compagnon. Je me voyais devant une foule exaspérée, en face du peloton d'exécution, pleurant du malheur qu'ils n'aient pu comprendre, et pardonnant!—Comme Jeanne d'Arc! —"Prêtres, professeurs, maîtres, vous vous trompez en me livrant à la justice. Je n'ai jamais été de ce peuple-ci; je n'ai jamais été chrétien; je suis de la race qui chantait dans le supplice; je ne comprends pas les lois; je n'ai pas le sens moral, je suis une brute: vous vous trompez."

Oui, j'ai les yeux fermés à votre lumière. Je suis une bête, un nègre. Mais je puis être sauvé. Vous êtes de faux nègres, vous, maniaques, féroces, avares.

heart: "Weakness or strength: there you are, it's strength. You do not know where you are going, nor why you are going; enter anywhere, reply to anything. They will no more kill you than if you were a corpse." In the morning I had a look so lost, a face so dead, that perhaps those whom I met *did not see me.*

In cities, suddenly, the mud seemed red and black like a mirror when the lamp moves about in the adjoining room, like a treasure in the forest! Good luck, I cried, and I saw a sea of flames and smoke in the sky; to the right, to the left all the riches of the world flaming like a billion thunder-bolts.

But to me debauch and the comradeship of women were denied. Not even a companion. I saw myself before an infuriated mob, facing the firing-squad, weeping out of pity for the evil they could not understand, and forgiving!—Like Jeanne d'Arc!—"Priests, professors, masters, you are making a mistake in turning me over to the law. I have never belonged to this people; I have never been a Christian; I am of the race that sang under torture; laws I have never understood; I have no moral sense, I am a brute: you are making a mistake."

Yes, my eyes are closed to your light. I am a beast, a nigger. But I can be saved. You are sham niggers, you, maniacs, fiends, misers. Merchant, you are

Marchand, tu es nègre; magistrat, tu es nègre; général, tu es nègre; empereur, vieille démangeaison, tu es nègre: tu as bu d'une liqueur non taxée, de la fabrique de Satan.—Ce peuple est inspiré par la fièvre et le cancer. Infirmes et vieillards sont tellement respectables qu'ils demandent à être bouillis.—Le plus malin est de quitter ce continent, où la folie rôde pour pourvoir d'otages ces misérables. J'entre au vrai royaume des enfants de Cham.

Connais-je encore la nature? me connais-je?—*Plus de mots*. J'ensevelis les morts dans mon ventre. Cris, tambour, danse, danse, danse, danse! Je ne vois même pas l'heure où, les blancs débarquant, je tomberai au néant.

Faim, soif, cris, danse, danse, danse, danse!

* * *

Les blancs débarquent. Le canon! Il faut se soumettre au baptême, s'habiller, travailler.

J'ai reçu au cœur le coup de la grâce. Ah! je ne l'avais pas prévu!

Je n'ai point fait le mal. Les jours vont m'être légers, le repentir me sera épargné. Je n'aurai pas eu les tourments de l'âme presque morte au bien, où remonte la lumière sévère comme les cierges funéraires. Le sort du fils de famille, cercueil prématuré couvert de limpides larmes. Sans doute la débauche est bête, le vice est bête; il faut jeter la

a nigger; Judge, you are a nigger; General, you are a nigger; Emperor, old itch, you are a nigger: you have drunk of the untaxed liquor of Satan's still.—Fever and cancer inspire this people. Cripples and old men are so respectable they are fit to be boiled.—The smartest thing would be to leave this continent where madness stalks to provide hostages for these wretches. I enter the true kingdom of the children of Ham.

Do I know nature yet? Do I know myself?—*No more words*. I bury the dead in my belly. Shouts, drums, dance, dance, dance, dance! I cannot even see the time when, white men landing, I shall fall into nothingness.

Hunger, thirst, shouts, dance, dance, dance, dance!

* * *

The white men are landing! The cannon! We must submit to baptism, put on clothes, work.

My heart has known the coup de grace. Ah! I did not foresee it.

I have never done evil. Light will my days be and I shall be spared repentance. I shall not have known the torments of the soul half dead to good, whence like funeral candles a grave light ascends. The fate of the sons of good families, the premature coffin covered with limpid tears. Certainly debauch is stupid, vice is stupid; all that is rotten must be cast

pourriture à l'écart. Mais l'horloge ne sera pas arrivée à ne plus sonner que l'heure de la pure douleur! Vais-je être enlevé comme un enfant, pour jouer au paradis dans l'oubli de tout le malheur?

Vite! est-il d'autres vies?—Le sommeil dans la richesse est impossible. La richesse a toujours été bien public. L'amour divin seul octroie les clefs de la science. Je vois que la nature n'est qu'un spectacle de bonté. Adieu chimères, idéals, erreurs!

Le chant raisonnable des anges s'élève du navire sauveur: c'est l'amour divin.—Deux amours! je puis mourir de l'amour terrestre, mourir de dévouement. J'ai laissé des âmes dont la peine s'accroîtra de mon départ! Vous me choisissez parmi les naufragés; ceux qui restent sont-ils pas mes amis?

Sauvez-les!

La raison m'est née. Le monde est bon. Je bénirai la vie. J'aimerai mes frères. Ce ne sont plus des promesses d'enfance. Ni l'espoir d'échapper à la vieillesse et à la mort. Dieu fait ma force et je loue Dieu.

* * *

L'ennui n'est plus mon amour. Les rages, les débauches, la folie,—dont je sais tous les élans et les désastres,—tout mon fardeau est déposé. Apprécions sans vertige l'étendue de mon innocence.

Je ne serais plus capable de demander le réconfort d'une bastonnade. Je ne me crois pas embarqué pour une noce avec Jésus-Christ pour beau-père.

aside. But the clock will not have succeeded in no longer striking only the hour of pure pain! Am I to be carried off like a child, to play in Paradise forgetful of all sorrow?

Quick! Are there other lives?—Sleep in wealth is impossible. Wealth has always been public property. The keys of knowledge are the gifts of divine love alone. I see that nature is but the display of goodness. Farewell chimeras, ideals, errors!

The reasonable song of angels rises from the saviour ship: it is divine love. Two loves! I can die of earthly love, die of devotion. I have abandoned souls whose pain will be increased by my going! Among the ship-wrecked you choose me; those who remain, are they not my friends?

Save them!

Reason is born to me. The world is good. I will bless life. I will love my brothers. These are no longer childish promises. Nor the hope of escaping old age and death. God is my strength and I praise God.

* * *

Boredom is no longer my love. Rages, debauchery, madness,—I have known all their soarings and their disasters,—My whole burden is laid down. Let us contemplate undazed the extent of my innocence. I would no longer be capable of begging the solace of a bastinado. I don't fancy myself embarked on a wedding with Jesus Christ as father-in-law.

Je ne suis pas prisonnier de ma raison. J'ai dit: Dieu. Je veux la liberté dans le salut: comment la poursuivre? Les goûts frivoles m'ont quitté. Plus besoin de dévouement ni d'amour divin. Je ne regrette pas le siècle des cœurs sensibles. Chacun a sa raison, mépris et charité: je retiens ma place au sommet de cette angélique échelle de bon sens.

Quant au bonheur établi, domestique ou non . . . non, je ne peux pas. Je suis trop dissipé, trop faible. La vie fleurit par le travail, vieille vérité: moi, ma vie n'est pas assez pesante, elle s'envole et flotte loin au-dessus de l'action, ce cher point du monde.

Comme je deviens vieille fille, à manquer du courage d'aimer la mort!

Si Dieu m'accordait le calme céleste, aérien, la prière,—comme les anciens saints.—Les saints, des forts! les anachorètes, des artistes comme il n'en faut plus!

Farce continuelle? Mon innocence me ferait pleurer. La vie est la farce à mener par tous.

* * *

Assez! voici la punition.—*En marche!*

Ah! les poumons brûlent, les tempes grondent! La nuit roule dans mes yeux, par ce soleil! Le cœur. . . les membres. . .

I am not a prisoner of my reason. I said: God. I want freedom in salvation: how am I to seek it? Frivolous tastes have left me. No more need of devotion or of divine love. No more regrets for the age of tender hearts. Each of us has his reason, scorn and charity; I reserve my place at the top of that angelic ladder of common sense.

As for established happiness, domestic or not. . . no, I cannot. I am too dissipated, too weak. Life flourishing through toil, old platitude! As for me, my life is not heavy enough, it flies and floats far above action, that precious focus of the world.

What an old maid I am getting to be, lacking the courage to be in love with death!

If only God would grant me celestial, aerial calm, prayer,—like the ancient Saints.—Saints, giants! anchorites, artists such as are not wanted any more!

Farce without end? My innocence would make me weep. Life is the farce we all have to lead.

* * *

Enough! Here is the punishment.—*Forward, march!*

Ah! My lungs are on fire, my temples roar! In this sunlight night rolls through my eyes: Heart. . . limbs. . .

Ou va-t-on? au combat? Je suis faible! les autres avancent. Les outils, les armes... le temps! ...

Feu! feu sur moi! Là! ou je me rends.—Lâches! —Je me tue! Je me jette aux pieds des chevaux!

Ah! ...

—Je m'y habituerai.

Ce serait la vie française, le sentier de l'honneur!

Where are we going? To battle? I am weak! The others advance. Tools, weapons. . . time! . . .

Fire! Fire on me! Here! Or I surrender.—Cowards! —I'll kill myself! I'll throw myself under the horses' hoofs!

Ah! . . .

—I shall get used to it.

It would be the French way of life, the path of honor!

NUIT DE L'ENFER

J'ai avalé une fameuse gorgée de poison.—Trois fois béni soit le conseil qui m'est arrivé!—Les entrailles me brûlent. La violence du venin tord mes membres, me rend difforme, me terrasse. Je meurs de soif, j'étouffe, je ne puis crier. C'est l'enfer, l'éternelle peine! Voyez comme le feu se relève! Je brûle comme il faut. Va, démon!

J'avais entrevu la conversion au bien et au bonheur, le salut. Puis-je décrire la vision? l'air de l'enfer ne souffre pas les hymnes! C'étaient des millions de créatures charmantes, un suave concert spirituel, la force et la paix, les nobles ambitions que sais-je?

Les nobles ambitions!

Et c'est encore la vie!—Si la damnation est éternelle! Un homme qui veut se mutiler est bien damné, n'est-ce pas? Je me crois en enfer, donc j'y suis. C'est

NIGHT OF HELL

I have swallowed a monstrous dose of poison.—Thrice blessed be the counsel that came to me!—My entrails are on fire. The violence of the venom twists my limbs, deforms and prostrates me. I die of thirst, I suffocate, and cannot scream. It is hell, eternal punishment! See how the fire flares up again! How nicely I burn. Go to it, demon!

I had caught a glimpse of conversion to good and to happiness, salvation. Can I describe the vision? The air of Hell will tolerate no hymns! There were a million charming creatures, a melodious sacred concert, strength and peace, noble ambitions—I don't know what all!

Noble ambitions!

And still this is life!—Suppose damnation were eternal! Then a man who would mutilate himself is well damned, isn't he? I think I am in hell, therefore I

l'exécution du catéchisme. Je suis esclave de mon baptême. Parents, vous avez fait mon malheur et vous avez fait le vôtre. Pauvre innocent!—L'enfer ne peut attaquer les païens.

—C'est la vie encore! Plus tard, les délices de la damnation seront plus profondes. Un crime, vite, que je tombe au néant, de par la loi humaine.

Tais-toi, mais tais-toi! . . . C'est la honte, le reproche, ici: Satan qui dit que le feu est ignoble, que ma colère est affreusement sotte.—Assez! . . . Des erreurs qu'on me souffle, magies, parfums faux, musiques puériles.—Et dire que je tiens la vérité, que je vois la justice: j'ai un jugement sain et arrêté, je suis prêt pour la perfection. . . Orgueil.—La peau de ma tête se dessèche. Pitié! Seigneur, j'ai peur. J'ai soif, si soif! Ah! l'enfance, l'herbe, la pluie, le lac sur les pierres, *le clair de lune quand le clocher sonnait douze*. . . Le diable est au clocher, à cette heure. Marie! Sainte Vierge! . . .—Horreur de ma bêtise.

Là-bas, ne sont-ce pas des âmes honnêtes, qui me veulent du bien? . . . Venez. . . J'ai un oreiller sur la bouche, elles ne m'entendent pas, ce sont des fantômes. Puis, jamais personne ne pense à autrui. Qu'on n'approche pas. Je sens le roussi, c'est certain.

Les hallucinations sont innombrables. C'est bien ce que j'ai toujours eu: plus de foi en l'histoire,

am in hell. It is the execution of the catechism. I am the slave of my baptism. Parents, you have been my undoing and your own. Poor innocent!—Hell has no power over pagans.

—This is life still! Later the delights of damnation will be more profound. A crime, quick, a crime, that I may fall into nothingness in accordance with human law.

Be quiet, do be quiet! . . . There's shame and reprobation here: Satan who says that the fire is contemptible, that my anger is horribly silly. Enough! . . . Fallacies they whisper to me, sorceries, false perfumes, childish music.—And to think that I possess truth, that I perceive justice: my judgment is sound and sure, I am ripe for perfection. . . Pride.—My scalp is drying up. Pity! Lord, I am afraid. I am thirsty, so thirsty! Ah, childhood, the grass, the rain, the lake over the stones, *the moonlight when the bell was chiming twelve*. . .the devil is in the belfry at this hour. Mary! Holy Virgin! . . .—Horror of my stupidity.

Out there, are they not honest souls that wish me well? . . . Come. . . I have a pillow over my mouth, they do not hear me, they are phantoms. Besides, no one ever thinks of others. Let no one come near me. I must smell scorched I'm sure.

Hallucinations are without number. Truly that is what I have always known: no more faith in history,

l'oubli des principes. Je m'en tairai: poètes et visionnaires seraient jaloux. Je suis mille fois le plus riche, soyons avare comme la mer.

Ah ça! l'horloge de la vie s'est arrêtée tout à l'heure. Je ne suis plus au monde.—La théologie est sérieuse, l'enfer est certainement *en bas,*—et le ciel en haut.—Extase, cauchemar, sommeil dans un nid de flammes.

Que de malices dans l'attention dans la campagne. . . Satan, Ferdinand, court avec les graines sauvages. . . Jésus marche sur les ronces purpurines, sans les courber. . . Jésus marchait sur les eaux irritées. La lanterne nous le montra debout, blanc et des tresses brunes, au flanc d'une vague d'émeraude. . .

Je vais dévoiler tous les mystères: mystères religieux ou naturels, mort, naissance, avenir, passé, cosmogonie, néant. Je suis maître en fantasmagories.

Ecoutez! . . .

J'ai tous les talents!—Il n'y a personne ici et il y a quel qu'un: je ne voudrais pas répandre mon trésor.—Veut-on des chants nègres, des danses de houris? Veut-on que je disparaisse, que je plonge à la recherche de l'*anneau?* Veut-on? Je ferai de l'or, des remèdes.

Fiez-vous donc à moi, la foi soulage, guide, guérit. Tous, venez,—même les petits enfants,—que je vous console, qu'on répande pour vous son cœur, le cœur

principles forgotten. I'll keep quiet about that: poets and visionaries would be jealous. I am a thousand times the richest, let us be as avaricious as the sea.

What! The clock of life stopped a while ago. I am no longer in the world.—Theology is serious, hell is certainly *down below*,—and heaven on high.—Ecstasy, nightmare, and sleep in a nest of flames.

What tricks of observation in the country. . . Satan, Old Nick, runs with the wild grain. . . Jesus walks on the purple briars and they do not bend. . . Jesus walked on the troubled waters. The lantern showed him to us, erect, white, with long brown hair, on the flank of an emerald wave. . . .

I am going to unveil all the mysteries: religious mysteries, or natural mysteries, death, birth, the future, the past, cosmogony, nothingness. I am a master of phantasmagoria.

Listen! . . .

I have all the talents!—There is no one here and there is someone: I would not squander my treasures. —Do you want negro songs, the dances of houris? Do you want me to vanish, to dive after the *ring?* Is that what you want? I will make gold, remedies.

Have faith in me then, faith assuages, guides, restores. Come, all of you—even the little children—that I may comfort you, that my heart may be poured

merveilleux!—Pauvres hommes, travailleurs! Je ne demande pas de prières; avec votre confiance seulement je serai heureux.

—Et pensons à moi. Ceci me fait peu regretter le monde. J'ai de la chance de ne pas souffrir plus. Ma vie ne fut que folies douces, c'est regrettable.

Bah! faisons toutes les grimaces imaginables.

Décidément, nous sommes hors du monde. Plus aucun son. Mon tact a disparu. Ah! mon château, ma Saxe, mon bois de saules. Les soirs, les matins, les nuits, les jours. . . Suis-je las!

Je devrais avoir mon enfer pour la colère, mon enfer pour l'orgueil,—et l'enfer de la paresse; un concert d'enfers.

Je meurs de lassitude. C'est le tombeau, je m'en vais aux vers, horreur de l'horreur! Satan, farceur, tu veux me dissoudre, avec tes charmes. Je réclame. Je réclame! un coup de fourche, une goutte de feu.

Ah! remonter à la vie! Jeter les yeux sur nos difformités. Et ce poison, ce baiser mille fois maudit! Ma faiblesse, la cruauté du monde! Mon Dieu, pitié, cachez-moi, je me tiens trop mal!—Je suis caché et je ne le suis pas.

C'est le feu qui se relève avec son damné.

out for you,—the marvelous heart!—Poor men, toilers! I do not ask for prayers; with your trust alone I shall be happy.

—And what of me? All this hardly makes me regret the world very much. I am lucky not to suffer more. My life was nothing but sweet follies, it's a pity.

Bah! Let's practice every imaginable grimace.

Decidedly we are out of the world. No longer any sound. My sense of touch has left me. Ah! my castle, my Saxony, my willow wood. Evenings, mornings, nights, days. . . How weary I am!

I should have my hell for anger, my hell for pride,—and the hell of laziness; a symphony of hells.

I die of lassitude. It is the tomb, I go to the worms, horror of horrors! Satan, you fraud, you would dissolve me with your charms. I insist. I insist! a thrust of the pitchfork, a drop of fire.

Ah! to rise again into life! to cast our eyes on our deformities. And that poison, that kiss, a thousand times accursed! My weakness, the cruelty of the world! My God, pity, hide me, I behave too badly!—I am hidden and I am not.

It is the fire that flares up again with its damned.

DELIRES

I

VIERGE FOLLE

L'ÉPOUX INFERNAL

Ecoutons la confession d'un compagnon d'enfer:

"O divin Epoux, mon Seigneur, ne refusez pas la confession de la plus triste de vos servantes. Je suis perdue. Je suis soûle. Je suis impure. Quelle vie!

"Pardon, divin Seigneur, pardon! Ah! pardon! Que de larmes! Et que de larmes encore plus tard, j'espère!

"Plus tard, je connaîtrai le divin Epoux! Je suis née soumise à Lui.—L'autre peut me battre maintenant!

DELIRIUM

I

THE FOOLISH VIRGIN

THE INFERNAL BRIDEGROOM

Let's hear now a hell-mate's confession:

"O heavenly Bridegroom, my Lord, do not reject the confession of the saddest of your handmaidens. I am lost. I am drunk. I am unclean. What a life!

"Forgive me, heavenly Lord, forgive me! Ah! forgive me! How many tears! And how many more tears later, I hope!

"Later I shall know the heavenly Bridegroom! I was born His slave.—The other can beat me now!

"A présent, je suis au fond du monde, ô mes amies! . . . non, pas mes amies. . . Jamais délires ni tortures semblables. . . Est-ce bête!

"Ah! je souffre, je crie. Je souffre vraiment. Tout pourtant m'est permis, chargée du mépris des plus méprisables cœurs.

"Enfin, faisons cette confidence, quitte à la répéter vingt autres fois,—aussi morne, aussi insignifiante!

"Je suis esclave de l'Epoux infernal, celui qui a perdu les vierges folles. C'est bien ce démon-là. Ce n'est pas un spectre, ce n'est pas un fantôme. Mais moi qui ai perdu la sagesse, qui suis damnée et morte au monde,—on ne me tuera pas! Comment vous le décrire! Je ne sais même plus parler. Je suis en deuil, je pleure, j'ai peur. Un peu de fraîcheur, Seigneur, si vous voulez, si vous voulez bien!

"Je suis veuve. . .—J'étais veuve. . .—mais oui, j'ai été bien sérieuse jadis, et je ne suis pas née pour devenir squelette! . . .—Lui était presque un enfant. . . . Ses délicatesses mystérieuses m'avaient séduite. J'ai oublié tout mon devoir humain pour le suivre. Quelle vie! La vraie vie est absente. Nous ne sommes pas au monde. Je vais où il va, il le faut. Et souvent il s'emporte contre moi, *moi, la pauvre âme*. Le Démon!—C'est un démon, vous savez, *ce n'est pas un homme*.

"At present I am at the bottom of the world! O my friends. . . no, not my friends. . . Never delirium and tortures like these. . . How stupid!

"Ah! I suffer, I scream. I really suffer. Yet everything is permitted me, burdened with the contempt of the most contemptible hearts.

"At any rate let me tell my secret, free to repeat it twenty times again,—just as dreary, just as insignificant!

"I am slave to the infernal Bridegroom, the one who was the undoing of the foolish virgins. He is really that very demon. He is not a ghost, he is not a phantom. But I who have lost all reason, who am damned and dead to the world,—they will not kill me! How describe him to you! I can no longer even speak. I am in mourning, I weep, I am afraid. A little coolness, Lord, if you will, if you only will!

"I am a widow. . .—I was a widow. . .—ah, yes, I was really serious once, and I was not born to be a skeleton! . . .—He was hardly more than a child. His mysterious delicacies had seduced me. I forgot all my duty to society, to follow him. What a life! Real life is absent. We are not in the world. I go where he goes, I have to. And often he flies into a rage at me, *me, the poor soul.* The Demon! He is a demon, you know, *he is not a man.*

"Il dit: 'Je n'aime pas les femmes: l'amour est à réinventer, on le sait. Elles ne peuvent plus que vouloir une position assurée. La position gagnée, cœur et beauté sont mis de côté: il ne reste que froid dédain, l'aliment du mariage, aujourd'hui. Ou bien je vois des femmes, avec les signes du bonheur, dont, moi, j'aurais pu faire de bonnes camarades, dévorées tout d'abord par des brutes sensibles comme des bûchers. . .'

"Je l'écoute faisant de l'infamie une gloire, de la cruauté un charme. 'Je suis de race lointaine: mes pères étaient Scandinaves; ils se perçaient les côtes, buvaient leur sang.—Je me ferai des entailles par tout le corps, je me tatouerai, je veux devenir hideux comme un Mongol: tu verras, je hurlerai dans les rues. Je veux devenir bien fou de rage. Ne me montre jamais de bijoux, je ramperais et me tordrais sur le tapis. Ma richesse, je la voudrais tachée de sang partout. Jamais je ne travaillerai. . .' Plusieurs nuits, son démon me saisissant, nous nous roulions, je luttais avec lui!—Les nuits, souvent, ivre, il se poste dans les rues ou dans des maisons, pour m'épouvanter mortellement.—'On me coupera vraiment le cou; ce sera dégoûtant.' Oh! ces jours où il veut marcher avec l'air du crime!

"Parfois il parle, en une façon de patois attendri, de la mort qui fait repentir, des malheureux qui

"He says: 'I do not like women: love must be reinvented, that's obvious. A secure position is all they're capable of desiring now. Security once gained, heart and beauty are set aside: cold disdain alone is left, the food of marriage today. Or else, I see women marked with the signs of happiness, and whom I could have made my comrades, promptly devoured by brutes with as much feeling as a log. . .'

"I listen to him glorifying infamy, clothing cruelty with charm. 'I am of a distant race: my ancestors were Norsemen; they used to pierce their sides, drink their blood.—I will cover myself with gashes, tattoo my body. I want to be as ugly as a Mongol: you'll see, I will howl through the streets. I want to become raving mad. Never show me jewels, I should grovel and writhe on the floor. My wealth, I'd want it spattered all over with blood. Never will I work. . .' Many nights his demon would seize me and rolling on the ground I would wrestle with him.—Often at night, drunk, he lies in wait for me, in streets, in houses, to frighten me to death.—'They will really cut my throat; it will be revolting.' Oh! those days when he goes wrapped in an air of crime!

"Sometimes he speaks in a kind of melting dialect, of death that brings repentance, of all the miserable

existent certainement, des travaux pénibles, des départs qui déchirent les cœurs. Dans les bouges où nous nous enivrions, il pleurait en considérant ceux qui nous entouraient, bétail de la misère. Il relevait les ivrognes dans les rues noires. Il avait la pitié d'une mère méchante pour les petits enfants.—Il s'en allait avec des gentillesse de petite fille au catéchisme.—Il feignait d'être éclairé sur tout, commerce, art, médecine.—Je le suivais, il le faut!

"Je voyais tout le décor dont, en esprit, il s'entourait: vêtements, draps, meubles; je lui prêtais des armes, une autre figure. Je voyais tout ce qui le touchait, comme il aurait voulu le créer pour lui. Quand il me semblait avoir l'esprit inerte, je le suivais, moi, dans des actions étranges et compliquées, loin, bonnes ou mauvaises: j'étais sûre de ne jamais entrer dans son monde. A côté de son cher corps endormi, que d'heures des nuits j'ai veillé, cherchant pourquoi il voulait tant s'évader de la réalité. Jamais homme n'eut pareil vœu. Je reconnaissais,—sans craindre pour lui,—qu'il pouvait être un sérieux danger dans la société.—Il a peut-être des secrets pour *changer la vie?* Non, il ne fait qu'en chercher, me répliquais-je. Enfin sa charité est ensorcelée, et j'en suis la prisonnière. Aucune autre âme n'aurait assez de force,—force de désespoir!—pour la supporter, pour être protégée et aimée par lui. D'ailleurs, je ne me le figurais

wretches there must be, of painful toil, of partings that lacerate the heart. In low dives where we'd get drunk, he used to weep for those around us, cattle of misery. He would lift up drunkards in the dark streets. He had the pity of a bad mother for little children.—He would depart with the graces of a little girl going to her catechism.—He pretended to have knowledge of everything, business, art, medicine.—I followed him, I had to!

"I saw the whole setting with which in his mind he surrounded himself: clothing, fabrics, furniture; I lent him arms, another face. I saw everything relating to him as he would have liked to create it for himself. When his mind seemed absent, I followed him, yes I, in strange and complicated actions, very far, good or bad: I was certain of never entering his world. How many hours of the night, beside his dear sleeping body I kept watch, trying to understand why he so longed to escape reality. Never a man had such a wish. I realized,—without any fear for him,—that he could be a serious danger to society. Perhaps he has some secrets for *changing life?* No, I would say to myself he is only looking for them. In short, his charity is bewitched, and I, its prisoner. No other soul would have enough strength—strength of despair!—to endure it, and to be protected and loved by him. Moreover, I never imagined him with another soul: one sees

pas avec une autre âme: on voit son Ange, jamais l'Ange d'un autre,—je crois. J'étais dans son âme comme dans un palais qu'on a vidé pour ne pas voir une personne si peu noble que vous: voilà tout. Hélas! je dépendais bien de lui. Mais que voulait-il avec mon existence terne et lâche? Il ne me rendait pas meilleure, s'il ne me faisait pas mourir! Tristement dépitée, je lui dis quelquefois: 'Je te comprends.' Il haussait les épaules.

"Ainsi, mon chagrin se renouvelant sans cesse, et me trouvant plus égarée à mes yeux,—comme à tous les yeux qui auraient voulu me fixer, si je n'eusse été condamnée pour jamais à l'oubli de tous!—j'avais de plus en plus faim de sa bonté. Avec ses baisers et ses étreintes amies, c'était bien un ciel, un sombre ciel, où j'entrais, et où j'aurais voulu être laissée, pauvre, sourde, muette, aveugle. Déjà j'en prenais l'habitude. Je nous voyais comme deux bons enfants, libres de se promener dans le Paradis de tristesse. Nous nous accordions. Bien émus, nous travaillions ensemble. Mais, après une pénétrante caresse, il disait: 'Comme ça te paraîtra drôle, quand je n'y serai plus, ce par quoi tu as passé. Quand tu n'auras plus mes bras sous ton cou, ni mon cœur pour t'y reposer, ni cette bouche sur tes yeux. Parce qu'il faudra que je m'en aille, très loin, un jour. Puis il faut que j'en aide d'autres: c'est mon devoir. Quoique ce ne soit guère ragoûtant. . .

one's own Angel, never the Angel of another—I believe. I was in his soul as in a palace they had emptied, so that no one should see so mean a person as oneself: that was all. Alas! I was really dependent on him. But what could he want with my dull, my craven life? He was making me no better if he wasn't driving me to death! Sometimes, chagrined and sad, I said to him: 'I understand you.' He would shrug his shoulders.

"Thus my sorrow always renewed, and seeming in my eyes more lost than ever,—as in the eyes of all who might have watched me had I not been condemned to be forgotten by all forever!—I hungered for his kindness more and more. With his kisses and his friendly arms, it was really heaven, a sombre heaven into which I entered and where I longed to be left, poor and deaf and dumb and blind. Already it had grown into a habit. I thought of us as two good children, free to wander in the Paradise of sadness. We were congenial to each other. Much moved, we used to work together. But after a profound caress he would say: 'How queer it will seem to you when I am no longer here—all you have gone through. When you no longer have my arm beneath your head, nor my heart for resting place, nor these lips upon your eyes. For I shall have to go away, very far away, one day. After all I must help others too: it is my duty. Not that it's very tempting. . . dear heart. . .' Right

chère âme. . .' Tout de suite je me pressentais, lui parti, en proie au vertige, précipitée dans l'ombre la plus affreuse: la mort. Je lui faisais promettre qu'il ne me lâcherait pas. Il l'a faite vingt fois, cette promesse d'amant. C'était aussi frivole que moi lui disant: 'Je te comprends.'

"Ah! je n'ai jamais été jalouse de lui. Il ne me quittera pas, je crois. Que devenir? Il n'a pas une connaissance; il ne travaillera jamais. Il veut vivre somnambule. Seules, sa bonté et sa charité lui donneraient-elles droit dans le monde réel? Par instants, j'oublie la pitié où je suis tombée: lui me rendra forte, nous voyagerons, nous chasserons dans les déserts, nous dormirons sur les pavés des villes inconnues, sans soins, sans peines. Ou je me réveillerai, et les lois et les mœurs auront changé,—grâce à son pouvoir magique; ou le monde, en restant le même, me laissera à mes désirs, joies, nonchalances. Oh! la vie d'aventures qui existe dans les livres des enfants, pour me récompenser, j'ai tant souffert, me la donneras-tu? Il ne peut pas. J'ignore son idéal. Il m'a dit avoir des regrets, des espoirs: cela ne doit pas me regarder. Parle-t-il à Dieu? Peut-être devrais-je m'adresser à Dieu. Je suis au plus profond de l'abîme, et je ne sais plus prier.

"S'il m'expliquait ses tristesses, les comprendrais-je plus que ses railleries? Il m'attaque, il passe des heures

away I saw myself, with him gone, my senses reeling, hurled into the most horrible darkness: death. I used to make him promise never to leave me. He made it twenty times, that lovers' promise. It was as vain as when I said to him: 'I understand you.'

"Ah! I have never been jealous of him. He will not leave me, I believe. What would become of him? He knows nothing; he will never work. He wants to live a sleep walker. Would his goodness and his charity alone give him the right to live in the real world? There are moments when I forget the abjection to which I have fallen; he will make me strong, we will travel, hunt in the deserts, we will sleep on the pavements of unknown cities, uncared for and without a care. Or else I shall awake, and the laws and customs will have changed,—thanks to his magic power,—or the world, while remaining the same, will leave me to my desires, joys, heedlessness. Oh! the life of adventure in childrens' books, to recompense me, I have suffered so, will you give me that? He cannot. His ideal is unknown to me. He has told me he has regrets, hopes: they can't have anything to do with me. Does he talk to God? I should appeal to God, perhaps. I am in the lowest depths, and I can no longer pray.

"If he explained his sadness to me, would I understand it any more than his mockery? He assails me,

à me faire honte de tout ce qui m'a pu toucher au monde, et s'indigne si je pleure.

—" 'Tu vois cet élégant jeune homme, entrant dans la belle et calme maison: il s'appelle Duval, Dufour, Armand, Maurice, que sais-je? Une femme s'est dévouée à aimer ce méchant idiot: elle est morte, c'est certes une sainte au ciel, à présent. Tu me feras mourir comme il a fait mourir cette femme. C'est notre sort, à nous cœurs charitables. . .' Hélas! Il y avait des jours où tous les hommes agissant lui paraissaient les jouets de délires grotesques; il riait affreusement, longtemps. —Puis, il reprenait ses manières de jeune mère, de sœur aînée. S'il était moins sauvage, nous serions sauvés! Mais sa douceur aussi est mortelle. Je lui suis soumise.—Ah! je suis folle!

"Un jour peut-être il disparaîtra merveilleusement; mais il faut que je sache, s'il doit remonter à un ciel, que je voie un peu l'assomption de mon petit ami!"

Drôle de ménage!

he spends hours making me ashamed of everything in the world that may have touched me, and is indignant if I weep.

" 'You see that elegant young man going into the beautiful, calm house; his name is Duval, Dufour, Armand, Maurice, or God knows what! A woman has devoted her life to loving that wicked idiot: she is dead, she must be a saint in heaven now. You will kill me as he has killed that woman. It is our lot, the lot of us, charitable hearts. . . !' Alas! he had days when all busy men seemed to him grotesque playthings of delirium; he would laugh long and horribly. Then he would revert to his manners of a young mother, a big sister. If he were less untamed we should be saved! But his tenderness too is deadly. I am his slave.—Ah! I am mad!

"One day, perhaps, he will miraculously disappear; but I must know if he is to ascend into some heaven again, so that I'll be sure not to miss the assumption of my little lover!"

Queer couple!

DELIRES

II

ALCHIMIE DU VERBE

A moi. L'histoire d'une de mes folies.

Depuis longtemps je me vantais de posséder tous les paysages possibles, et trouvais dérisoires les célébrités de la peinture et de la poésie modernes.

J'aimais les peintures idiotes, dessus de porte, décors, toiles de saltimbanques, enseignes, enluminures populaires; la littérature démodée, latin d'église, livres érotiques sans orthographe, romans de nos aïeules, contes de fées, petits livres de l'enfance, opéras vieux, refrains niais, rhythmes naïfs.

Je rêvais croisades, voyages de découvertes dont on n'a pas de relations, républiques sans histoires, guerres

DELIRIUM

II

ALCHEMY OF THE WORD

Now for me! The story of one of my follies.

For a long time I boasted of possessing every possible landscape and held in derision the celebrities of modern painting and poetry.

I loved maudlin pictures, the painted panels over doors, stage sets, the back-drops of mountebanks, old inn signs, popular prints; antiquated literature, church Latin, erotic books innocent of all spelling, the novels of our grandfathers, fairytales, children's storybooks, old operas, inane refrains and artless rhythms.

I dreamed crusades, unrecorded voyages of discovery, untroubled republics, religious wars stifled, revo-

de religion étouffées, révolutions de mœurs, déplacements de races et de continents: je croyais à tous les enchantements.

J'inventai la couleur des voyelles!—*A* noir, *E* blanc, *I* rouge, *O* bleu, *U* vert.—Je réglai la forme et le mouvement de chaque consonne, et, avec des rhythmes instinctifs, je me flattai d'inventer un verbe poétique accessible, un jour ou l'autre, à tous les sens. Je réservais la traduction.

Ce fut d'abord une étude. J'écrivais des silences, des nuits, je notais l'inexprimable. Je fixais des vertiges.

* * *

Loin des oiseaux, des troupeaux, des villageoises,
Que buvais-je, à genoux dans cette bruyère
Entourée de tendres bois de noisetiers,
Dans un brouillard d'après-midi tiède et vert?

Que pouvais-je boire dans cette jeune Oise,
—Ormeaux sans voix, gazon sans fleurs, ciel couvert!—
Boire à ces gourdes jaunes, loin de ma case
Chérie? Quelque liqueur d'or qui fait suer.

lutions of customs, the displacements of races and continents: I believed in all marvels.

I invented the color of vowels!—*A* black, *E* white, *I* red, *O* blue, *U* green.—I regulated the form and the movement of every consonant, and with instinctive rhythms I prided myself on inventing a poetic language accessible some day to all the senses. I reserved all rights of translation.

At first it was an experiment. I wrote silences, I wrote the night. I recorded the inexpressible. I fixed frenzies in their flight.

* * *

Far from birds and flocks and village girls,
What did I drink as I knelt in the heather,
A tender hazel copse around me,
In the warm green mist of the afternoon?

What could I drink in that young Oise,
—Voiceless the trees, flowerless the grass, sky overcast!—
Drink at those yellow gourds far from my cabin
So dear? Liquors of gold that bring heavy sweating.

Je faisais une louche enseigne d'auberge.
—Un orage vint chasser le ciel. Au soir
L'eau des bois se perdait sur les sables vierges,
Le vent de Dieu jetait des glaçons aux mares;

Pleurant, je voyais de l'or,—et ne pus boire.

* * *

A quatre heures du matin, l'été,
Le sommeil d'amour dure encore.
Sous les bocages s'évapore
  L'odeur du soir fêté.

Là-bas, dans leur vaste chantier,
Au soleil des Hespérides,
Déjà s'agitent—en bras de chemise—
  Les Charpentiers.

Dans leurs Déserts de mousse, tranquilles,
Ils préparent les lambris précieux
    Où la ville
  Peindra de faux cieux.

O, pour ces Ouvriers, charmants
Sujets d'un roi de Babylone,
Vénus! quitte un instant les Amants
  Dont l'âme est en couronne!

I seemed a sorry sign for an inn.
—A storm came chasing the sky away. And virgin
sands
Drank all the water of the evening woods,
God's wind blew icicles into the ponds;

As I wept I saw gold,—and could not drink.

* * *

Morning, summer, four o'clock,
Deep still love's sleep endures.
While feted evening's odors
From the green bowers evaporate.

Down in their vast woodyards,
Under an Hesperian sun,
The Carpenters—in shirt sleeves—
Toil already;

Calm in their Deserts of moss,
Precious canopies preparing,
Where the city will paint
Skies fabulous and false.

O, for those charming Workers,
Subjects of a Babylonian king,
Venus! a moment leave the Lovers
Whose souls are wreathed!

O Reine des Bergers,
Porte aux travailleurs l'eau-de-vie,
Que leurs forces soient en paix
En attendant le bain dans la mer à midi.

* * *

La vieillerie poétique avait une bonne part dans mon alchimie du verbe.

Je m'habituai à l'hallucination simple: je voyais très franchement une mosquée à la place d'une usine, une école de tambours faite par des anges, des calèches sur les routes du ciel, un salon au fond d'un lac; les monstres, les mystères; un titre de vaudeville dressait des épouvantes devant moi.

Puis j'expliquai mes sophismes magiques avec l'hallucination des mots!

Je finis par trouver sacré le désordre de mon esprit. J'étais oisif, en proie à une lourde fièvre: j'enviais la félicité des bêtes,—les chenilles, qui représentent l'innocence des limbes, les taupes, le sommeil de la virginité!

Mon caractère s'aigrissait. Je disais adieu au monde dans d'espèces de romances:

O queen of Shepherds,
Bring to the workers wine,
That their powers be appeased
Awaiting the noon swim in the sea.

* * *

Poetic quaintness played a large part in my alchemy of the word.

I became an adept at simple hallucination: in place of a factory I really saw a mosque, a school of drummers led by angels, carriages on the highways of the sky, a drawing-room at the bottom of a lake; monsters, mysteries; the title of a melodrama would raise horrors before me.

Then I would explain my magic sophisms with the hallucination of words!

Finally I came to regard as sacred the disorder of my mind. I was idle, full of a sluggish fever: I envied the felicity of beasts, caterpillars that represent the innocence of limbo, moles, the sleep of virginity!

My temper soured. In kinds of ballads I said farewell to the world:

CHANSON DE LA PLUS HAUTE TOUR

Qu'il vienne, qu'il vienne,
Le temps dont on s'éprenne.

J'ai tant fait patience
Qu'à jamais j'oublie.
Craintes et souffrances
Aux cieux sont parties.
Et la soif malsaine
Obscurcit mes veines.

Qu'il vienne, qu'il vienne,
Le temps dont on s'éprenne.

Telle la prairie
A l'oubli livrée,
Grandie et fleurie
D'encens et d'ivraies,
Au bourdon farouche
De sales mouches.

Qu'il vienne, qu'il vienne,
Le temps dont on s'éprenne.

SONG OF THE HIGHEST TOWER

O may it come, the time of love,
The time we'd be enamoured of.

I've been patient too long,
My memory is dead,
All fears and all wrongs
To the heavens have fled.
While all my veins burst
With a sickly thirst.

O may it come, the time of love,
The time we'd be enamoured of.

Like the meadow that is dreaming
Forgetful of cares,
Flourishing and flowering
With incense and tares,
Where fierce buzzings rise
Of filthy flies.

O may it come, the time of love,
The time we'd be enamoured of.

J'aimai le désert, les vergers brûlés, les boutiques fanées, les boissons tiédies. Je me traînais dans les ruelles puantes et, les yeux fermés, je m'offrais au soleil, dieu de feu.

"Général, s'il reste un vieux canon sur tes remparts en ruines, bombarde-nous avec des blocs de terre sèche. Aux glaces des magasins splendides! dans les salons! Fais manger sa poussière à la ville. Oxyde les gargouilles. Emplis les boudoirs de poudre de rubis brûlante. . ."

Oh! le moucheron enivré à la pissotière de l'auberge, amoureux de la bourrache, et que dissout un rayon!

FAIM

Si j'ai du goût, ce n'est guères
Que pour la terre et les pierres.
Je déjeune toujours d'air,
De roc, de charbons, de fer.

Mes faims, tournez. Paissez, faims,
Le pré des sons.
Attirez le gai venin
Des liserons.

I loved the desert, dried orchards, faded shops and tepid drinks. I dragged myself through stinking alleys and, eyes closed, I gave myself to the sun, God of fire.

"General, if on your ruined ramparts an old cannon remains, bombard us with lumps of dried mud.—On the mirrors of magnificent shops! in drawing-rooms! Make the city eat its dust. Oxidize the water-spouts. Fill boudoirs with the burning powder of rubies. . ."

Oh! the drunken fly in the inn's privy, enamoured of borage, dissolved by a sunbeam!

HUNGER

If I've a taste, it's not alone
For the earth and stones,
Rocks, coal, iron, air,
That's my daily fare.

Turn my hungers, hungers browse
On the field of sound,
Suck up bindweed's gay venom
Along the ground.

Mangez les cailloux qu'on brise,
Les vieilles pierres d'églises;
Les galets des vieux déluges,
Pains semés dans les vallées grises.

* * *

Le loup criait sous les feuilles
En crachant les belles plumes
De son repas de volailles:
Comme lui je me consume.

Les salades, les fruits
N'attendent que la cueillette;
Mais l'araignée de la haie
Ne mange que des violettes.

Que je dorme! que je bouille
Aux autels de Salomon.
Le bouillon court sur la rouille,
Et se mêle au Cédron.

Enfin, ô bonheur, ô raison, j'écartai du ciel l'azur, qui est du noir, et je vécus, étincelle d'or de la lumière *nature*. De joie, je prenais une expression bouffonne et égarée au possible:

* * *

Eat the pebbles that one breaks,
Churches' old stones;
Gravel of ancient deluge taste,
And loaves scattered in grey brakes.

* * *

Howling underneath the leaves
The wolf spits out the lovely plumes
Of his feast of fowls:
Like him I am consumed.

Salads and fruits
Await but the picking;
But violets are the food
Of spiders in the thicket.

Let me sleep! Let me seethe
At the altars of Solomon.
Broth run over the rust
And mix with the Cedron.

At last, O happiness, O reason, I brushed from the sky the azure that is darkness, and I lived—gold spark of *pure* light. Out of joy I took on an expression as clownish and blank as possible:

* * *

Elle est retrouvée!
Quoi? l'Eternité.
C'est la mer mêlée
Au soleil.

Mon âme éternelle,
Observe ton vœu
Malgré la nuit seule
Et le jour en feu.

Donc tu te dégage
Des humains suffrages,
Des communs élans!
Tu voles selon. . .

Jamais l'espérance,
Pas d'*orietur*.
Science et patience,
Le supplice est sûr.

Plus de lendemain,
Braises de satin,
Votre ardeur
Est le devoir.

Elle est retrouvée!
—Quoi?—l'Eternité.
C'est la mer mêlée
Au soleil.

It is recovered!
What? Eternity.
It is the sea
Mixed with the sun.

My soul eternal,
Redeem your promise,
In spite of the night alone
And the day on fire.

Of human suffrage,
Of common aspirings,
You free yourself then!
You fly according to. . .

Hope never more,
No *orietur.*
Science and patience,
Retribution is sure.

No more tomorrows,
Embers of satin,
Your ardor is now
Your duty only.

It is recovered!
What? Eternity.
It is the sea
Mixed with the sun.

Je devins un opéra fabuleux: je vis que tous les êtres ont une fatalité de bonheur: l'action n'est pas la vie, mais une façon de gâcher quelque force, un énervement. La morale est la faiblesse de la cervelle.

A chaque être, plusieurs *autres* vies me semblaient dues. Ce monsieur ne sait ce qu'il fait: il est un ange. Cette famille est une nichée de chiens. Devant plusieurs hommes, je causai tout haut avec un moment d'une de leurs autres vies.—Ainsi, j'ai aimé un porc.

Aucun des sophismes de la folie,—la folie qu'on enferme,—n'a été oublié par moi: je pourrais les redire tous, je tiens le système.

Ma santé fut menacée. La terreur venait. Je tombais dans des sommeils de plusieurs jours, et, levé, je continuais les rêves les plus tristes. J'étais mûr pour le trépas, et par une route de dangers ma faiblesse me menait aux confins du monde et de la Cimmérie, patrie de l'ombre et des tourbillons.

Je dus voyager, distraire les enchantements assemblés dans mon cerveau. Sur la mer, que j'aimais comme si elle eût dû me laver d'une souillure, je voyais se lever la croix consolatrice. J'avais été damné par l'arc-en-ciel. Le Bonheur était ma fatalité, mon remords, mon ver: ma vie serait toujours trop immense pour être dévouée à la force et à la beauté.

Le Bonheur! Sa dent, douce à la mort, m'avertissait au chant du coq,—*ad matutinum*, au *Christus venit*,—dans les plus sombres villes:

I became a fabulous opera; I saw that all creatures have a fatality of happiness: action is not life, but only a way of spoiling some force, an enervation. Morality is the weakness of the brain.

It seemed to me that to every creature several *other* lives were due. This gentleman knows not what he does: he is an angel. This family is a litter of puppies. With several men I have spoken aloud with a moment of one of their other lives. Thus it was I loved a pig.

Not a single sophistry of madness—madness to be confined—was forgotten: I could recite them all again, I know the system.

My health was threatened. Terror came. I would fall into a slumber of days, and getting up would go on with the same sad dreams. I was ripe for death and along a road of perils my weakness led me to the confines of the world and of Cimmeria, home of whirlwinds and of darkness.

I had to travel, divert the spells assembled in my brain. Over the sea, that I loved as though it were to cleanse me of a stain, I saw the comforting cross arise. I had been damned by the rainbow. Happiness was my fatality, my remorse, my worm: my life would always be too enormous to be devoted to strength and to beauty.

Happiness! Its tooth deadly sweet, warned me at the crowing of the cock,—*ad matutinum,* at the *Christus venit,*—in the darkest cities:

O saisons, ô châteaux!
Quelle âme est sans défauts!

J'ai fait la magique étude
Du bonheur, qu'aucun n'élude.

Salut à lui chaque fois
Que chante le coq gaulois.

Ah! je n'aurai plus d'envie:
Il s'est chargé de ma vie.

Ce charme a pris âme et corps
Et dispersé les efforts.

O saisons, ô châteaux!

L'heure de la fuite, hélas!
Sera l'heure du trépas.

O saisons, ô châteaux!

* * *

Cela s'est passé. Je sais aujourd'hui saluer la beauté.

O seasons, O castles!
What soul is without sin!

The magic study I've made,
Of happiness none can evade.

To it each time, good luck,
We hear the Gallic cock.

No more desires for me:
It has taken my life in fee.

Charmed body, soul and brain
Delivered of every strain.

O seasons, O castles!

The hour of flight will be
The hour of death for me!

O seasons, O castles!

* * *

That is over. Now I know how to salute beauty.

L'IMPOSSIBLE

Ah! cette vie de mon enfance, la grande route par tous les temps, sobre surnaturellement, plus désintéressé que le meilleur des mendiants, fier de n'avoir ni pays, ni amis, quelle sottise c'était.—Et je m'en aperçois seulement!

—J'ai eu raison de mépriser ces bonshommes qui ne perdraient pas l'occasion d'une caresse, parasites de la propreté et de la santé de nos femmes, aujourd'hui qu'elles sont si peu d'accord avec nous.

J'ai eu raison dans tous mes dédains: puisque je m'évade!

Je m'évade?

Je m'explique.

Hier encore, je soupirais: "Ciel! sommes-nous assez de damnés ici-bas! Moi, j'ai tant de temps déjà dans leur troupe! Je les connais tous. Nous nous recon-

THE IMPOSSIBLE

Ah! That life of my childhood, the highroad in all weathers, supernaturally sober, more disinterested than the best of beggars, proud to have neither country, nor friends, how stupid it was! And I see it only now!

—I was right to despise those poor fellows who would never miss the chance of a caress, parasites of the cleanliness and health of our women, now that they are so little in accord with us.

I was right in all my contempts: since I escape.

I escape?

I'll explain.

Yesterday I was still sighing: "Heavens! aren't there enough of us damned ones here below! How long I've spent already in their troupe! I know them all. We recognize each other always; we disgust

naissons toujours; nous nous dégoûtons. La charité nous est inconnue. Mais nous sommes polis; nos relations avec le monde sont très convenables." Est-ce étonnant? Le monde! les marchands, les naïfs!—Nous ne sommes pas déshonorés.—Mais les élus, comment nous recevraient-ils? Or il y a des gens hargneux et joyeux, de faux élus, puisqu'il nous faut de l'audace ou de l'humilité pour les aborder. Ce sont les seuls élus. Ce ne sont pas des bénisseurs!

M'étant retrouvé deux sous de raison,—ça passe vite!—je vois que mes malaises viennent de ne m'être pas figuré assez tôt que nous sommes à l'Occident. Les marais occidentaux! Non que je croie la lumière altérée, la forme exténuée, le mouvement égaré. . . Bon! voici que mon esprit veut absolument se charger de tous les développements cruels qu'a subis l'esprit depuis la fin de l'Orient. . . Il en veut, mon esprit!

. . . Mes deux sous de raison sont finis!—L'esprit est autorité, il veut que je sois en Occident. Il faudrait le faire taire pour conclure comme je voulais.

J'envoyais au diable les palmes des martyrs, les rayons de l'art, l'orgueil des inventeurs, l'ardeur des pillards; je retournais à l'Orient et à la sagesse première et éternelle.—Il paraît que c'est un rêve de paresse grossière!

Pourtant, je ne songeais guère au plaisir d'échapper aux souffrances modernes. Je n'avais pas en vue la sagesse bâtarde du Coran.—Mais n'y a-t-il pas un

each other. Charity is unknown to us. But we are civil; our relations with the world are most correct." Is it surprising? The world! tradesmen, simple souls!—We are not dishonored.—But the elect, how would they receive us? Now, there are the surly and joyous ones, the false elect, since we need daring or humility to approach them. They are the only elect. They are not those who bless!

Having recovered two cents worth of reason,—it is soon gone!—I see that my disquietudes come from having understood too late that we are in the Occident. Occidental swamps! Not that I think light faded, form shrunk, movement lost. . . Well! here is my spirit insisting on taking upon itself all the cruel developments that the spirit has suffered since the end of the Orient. . . It really insists, my spirit!

. . . My two cents worth of reason is spent! Spirit is in command, it insists that I be in the Occident. I'd have to silence it to conclude as I wished.

To the devil, I said, with martyrs' crowns, the beams of art, the pride of inventors, the ardor of plunderers; I returned to the Orient and to the first and eternal wisdom.—A dream of vulgar indolence it would seem!

Yet, I was hardly thinking of the pleasure of escaping modern wretchedness. I was not thinking of the bastard wisdom of the Koran.—But is there not real

supplice réel en ce que, depuis cette déclaration de la science, le christianisme, l'homme *se joue*, se prouve les évidences, se gonfle du plaisir de répéter ces preuves, et ne vit que comme cela? Torture subtile, niaise; source de mes divagations spirituelles. La nature pourrait s'ennuyer, peut-être! M. Prudhomme * est né avec le Christ.

N'est-ce pas parce que nous cultivons la brume? Nous mangeons la fièvre avec nos légumes aqueux. Et l'ivrognerie! et le tabac! et l'ignorance! et les dévouements!—Tout cela est-il assez loin de la pensée, de la sagesse de l'Orient, la patrie primitive? Pourquoi un monde moderne, si de pareils poisons s'inventent!

Les gens d'Eglise diront: C'est compris. Mais vous voulez parler de l'Eden. Rien pour vous dans l'histoire des peuples orientaux.—C'est vrai; c'est à l'Eden que je songeais! Qu'est-ce que c'est pour mon rêve, cette pureté des races antiques!

Les philosophes: Le monde n'a pas d'âge. L'humanité se déplace, simplement. Vous êtes en Occident, mais libre d'habiter dans votre Orient, quelque ancien qu'il vous le faille,—et d'y habiter bien. Ne

* *Monsieur Prudhomme:* a character created by Henri Monnier (1857) frequently referred to in French literature. Solemnly and ostentatiously banal, he is the prototype of the smug bourgeois who is a reflection of his environment. He has a taste for meaningless grandiloquence, is always pompously "proving the obvious" and un-

torment in this that, ever since that declaration of science, Christianity, man *fools himself,* proves to himself the obvious, puffs himself up with the pleasure of reiterating those proofs, and can live in no other way! Subtle, silly torture; source of all my spiritual vagrancies. Nature can be bored, perhaps! Monsieur Prudhomme * was born with Christ.

Is it not because we cultivate fog! We eat fever with our watery vegetables. And drunkenness! and tobacco! and ignorance! and self-sacrifice!—How far all this is from the conception, from the wisdom of the Orient, the original fatherland! Why a modern world if such poisons are invented!

Churchmen will say: Granted. But you mean Eden. Nothing for you in the history of Oriental peoples.—It is true; it is of Eden I was thinking! What has it to do with my dream—that purity of ancient races!

Philosophers: The world has no age. Humanity simply changes place. You are in the Occident, but free to live in your Orient, as ancient as you please,

consciously trying to convince himself and others that he is not a nonentity. The name is a satiric reference to the meaning of the word, *prud'homme,* righteous man. This self-righteous mediocrity, Rimbaud says, "was born with Christ," and for mediocrity Rimbaud reserved his bitterest "contempt" and passionate hatred.

soyez pas un vaincu. Philosophes, vous êtes de votre Occident.

Mon esprit, prends garde. Pas de partis de salut violents. Exerce-toi!—Ah! la science ne va pas assez vite pour nous!

—Mais je m'aperçois que mon esprit dort.

S'il était bien éveillé toujours à partir de ce moment, nous serions bientôt à la vérité, qui peut-être nous entoure avec ses anges pleurant! . . .—S'il avait été éveillé jusqu'à ce moment-ci, c'est que je n'aurais pas cédé aux instincts délétères, à une époque immémoriale! . . .—S'il avait toujours été bien éveillé, je voguerais en pleine sagesse! . . .

O pureté! pureté!

C'est cette minute d'éveil qui m'a donné la vision de la pureté!—Par l'esprit on va à Dieu!

Déchirante infortune!

and to live well. Don't admit defeat. Philosophers, you are of your Occident.

My spirit, beware. No violent projects of salvation. Bestir yourself!—Ah! for us science is too slow!

—But I see that my spirit is asleep.

If it were always wide awake from that moment on we should soon reach the truth that may even now surround us with her weeping angels! . . .—If it had been awake till this very instant, that would mean I had not yielded to my deleterious instincts in an immemorial age! . . .—If it had always been wide awake, I should be under full sail on the high sea of wisdom! . . .

O purity! purity!

It is this moment of awakening that has given me the vision of purity!—Through the spirit we go to God!

Heart-breaking misfortune!

L'ECLAIR

Le travail humain! c'est l'explosion qui éclaire mon abîme de temps en temps.

"Rien n'est vanité; à la science, et en avant!" crie l'Ecclésiaste moderne, c'est-à-dire *Tout le monde*. Et pourtant les cadavres des méchants et des fainéants tombent sur le cœur des autres. . . Ah! vite, vite un peu; là-bas, par delà la nuit, ces récompenses futures, éternelles. . . les échapperons-nous?

—Qu'y puis-je? Je connais le travail; et la science est trop lente. Que la prière galope et que la lumière gronde. . . je le vois bien. C'est trop simple, et il fait trop chaud; on se passera de moi. J'ai mon devoir; j'en serai fier à la façon de plusieurs, en le mettant de côté.

Ma vie est usée. Allons! feignons, fainéantons, ô pitié! Et nous existerons en nous amusant, en rêvant

LIGHTNING FLASH

Human toil! That is the explosion which lights up my abyss from time to time.

"Nothing is vanity; all for science and forward!" cries the modern Ecclesiastes, that is to say *Everybody*. And yet the corpses of the wicked and the sluggards fall on the hearts of others. . . Ah! hurry, do hurry; out there, beyond the night, those future, those eternal rewards. . . shall we escape them? . . .

—What can I do? I know what toil is; and science is too slow. Let prayer gallop and light thunder. . . I see it clearly. It is too simple, and it's too hot; they will get along without me. I have my duty; I shall be proud of it after the fashion of several others by setting it aside.

My life is threadbare. All right! Let's sham and shirk, O pity! And we will go on enjoying ourselves,

amours monstres et univers fantastiques, en nous plaignant et en querellant les apparences du monde, saltimbanque, mendiant, artiste, bandit,—prêtre! Sur mon lit d'hôpital, l'odeur de l'encens m'est revenue si puissante: gardien des aromates sacrés, confesseur, martyr. . .

Je reconnais là ma sale éducation d'enfance. Puis quoi! . . . Aller mes vingt ans, si les autres vont vingt ans. . .

Non! non! à présent je me révolte contre la mort! Le travail paraît trop léger à mon orgueil: ma trahison au monde serait un supplice trop court. Au dernier moment, j'attaquerais à droite, à gauche. . .

Alors,—oh!—chère pauvre âme, l'éternité serait-elle pas perdue pour nous!

dreaming monstrous loves, fantastic universes, grumbling, and quarreling with the world's disguises, mountebank, beggar, artist, scoundrel. . . priest! On my hospital bed, the odor of incense came back to me so potent: guardian of the sacred aromatics, confessor, martyr. . .

There I recognize the filthy education of my childhood. What of it? . . . To go my twenty years, if others go their twenty years. . .

No! No! Now I rebel against death! Toil seems too trifling to my pride: my betrayal to the world would be too brief a torture. At the last moment I would strike out, to the right, to the left. . .

Then—oh!—dear, poor soul, would not eternity be lost to us!

MATIN

N'eus-je pas *une fois* une jeunesse aimable, héroïque, fabuleuse, à écrire sur des feuilles d'or, trop de chance! Par quel crime, par quelle erreur, ai-je mérité ma faiblesse actuelle? Vous qui prétendez que des bêtes poussent des sanglots de chagrin, que des malades désespèrent, que des morts rêvent mal, tâchez de raconter ma chute et mon sommeil. Moi, je ne puis pas plus m'expliquer que le mendiant avec ses continuels *Pater* et *Ave Maria. Je ne sais plus parler!*

Pourtant, aujourd'hui, je crois avoir fini la relation de mon enfer. C'était bien l'enfer; l'ancien, celui dont le fils de l'homme ouvrit les portes.

Du même désert, à la même nuit, toujours mes yeux las se réveillent à l'étoile d'argent, toujours, sans que s'émeuvent les Rois de la vie, les trois mages, le cœur, l'âme, l'esprit. Quand irons-nous, par delà les

MORNING

Had I not *once* a lovely youth, heroic, fabulous, to be written on sheets of gold, good luck and to spare! Through what crime, through what fault have I deserved my weakness now? You who declare that beasts sob in their grief, that the sick despair, that the dead have bad dreams, try to relate my fall and my sleep. As for me, I can no more explain myself than the beggar with his endless *Paters* and *Ave Marias. I can no longer speak!*

However, I have finished, I think, the tale of my hell today. It was really hell; the old hell, the one whose doors were opened by the son of man.

From the same desert, in the same night, always my tired eyes awake to the silver star, always, but the Kings of life are not moved, the three magi, mind and heart and soul. When shall we go beyond the

grèves et les monts, saluer la naissance du travail nouveau, la sagesse nouvelle, la fuite des tyrans et des démons, la fin de la superstition, adorer—les premiers! —Noël sur la terre?

Le chant des cieux, la marche des peuples! Esclaves, ne maudissons pas la vie.

mountains and the shores, to greet the birth of new toil, of new wisdom, the flight of tyrants, of demons, the end of superstitition, to adore—the first to adore! —Christmas on the earth.

The song of the heavens, the marching of peoples! Slaves, let us not curse life.

ADIEU

L'automne déjà!—Mais pourquoi regretter un éternel soleil, si nous sommes engagés à la découverte de la clarté divine,—loin des gens qui meurent sur les saisons.

L'automne. Notre barque élevée dans les brumes immobiles tourne vers le port de la misère, la cité énorme au ciel taché de feu et de boue. Ah! les haillons pcurris, le pain trempé de pluie, l'ivresse, les mille amours qui m'ont crucifié! Elle ne finira donc point cette goule reine de millions d'âmes et de corps morts *et qui seront jugés!* Je me revois, la peau rongée par la boue et la peste, des vers plein les cheveux et les aisselles et encore de plus gros vers dans le cœur, étendu parmi les inconnus sans âge, sans sentiment. . . J'aurais pu y mourir. . . L'affreuse évocation! J'exècre la misère.

FAREWELL

Autumn already!—But why regret an eternal sun if we are embarked on the discovery of divine light—far from all those who fret over seasons.

Autumn. Risen through the motionless mists, our boat turns toward the port of misery, the enormous city with fire-and-mud-stained sky. Ah, the putrid rags, the rain-soaked bread, drunkenness, the thousand loves that have crucified me! Will she never have done, then, that ghoul queen of a million dead souls and dead bodies, *and which will be judged!* I see myself again, skin rotten with mud and pest, worms in my armpits and in my hair, and in my heart much bigger worms, lying among strangers without age, without feeling... I might have died there... Unbearable evocation! I loathe poverty.

Et je redoute l'hiver parce que c'est la saison du confort!

—Quelquefois je vois au ciel des plages sans fin couvertes de blanches nations en joie. Un grand vaisseau d'or, au-dessus de moi, agite ses pavillons multicolores sous les brises du matin. J'ai créé toutes les fêtes, tous les triomphes, tous les drames. J'ai essayé d'inventer de nouvelles fleurs, de nouveaux astres, de nouvelles chairs, de nouvelles langues. J'ai cru acquérir des pouvoirs surnaturels. Eh bien! je dois enterrer mon imagination et mes souvenirs! Une belle gloire d'artiste et de conteur emportée!

Moi! moi qui me suis dit mage ou ange, dispensé de toute morale, je suis rendu au sol, avec un devoir à chercher, et la réalité rugueuse à étreindre! Paysan!

Suis-je trompé? La charité serait-elle sœur de la mort pour moi?

Enfin, je demanderai pardon pour m'être nourri de mensonge. Et allons.

Mais pas une main amie! et où puiser le secours?

* * *

Oui, l'heure nouvelle est au moins très sévère.

Car je puis dire que la victoire m'est acquise: les grincements de dents, les sifflements de feu, les soupirs empestés se modèrent. Tous les souvenirs immondes s'effacent. Mes derniers regrets détalent,—

And I dread winter because it is the season of comfort!

Sometimes in the sky I see endless beaches covered with white nations full of joy. Above me a great golden ship waves its multi-colored pennants in the breezes of the morning. I created all fêtes, all triumphs, all dramas. I tried to invent new flowers, new stars, new flesh, new tongues. I thought I was acquiring supernatural powers. Well! I must bury my imagination and my memories! An artist's and storyteller's precious fame flung away!

I! I who called myself angel or seer, exempt from all morality, I am returned to the soil with a duty to seek and rough reality to embrace! Peasant!

Am I mistaken? Would charity be the sister of death for me?

At last, I shall ask forgiveness for having fed on lies. And now let's go.

But no friendly hand! And where turn for help!

* * *

Yes, the new hour is at least very severe.

For I can say that victory is won: the gnashing of teeth, the hissings of fire, the pestilential sighs are abating. All the noisome memories are fading. My last regrets take to their heels,—envy of beggars,

des jalousies pour les mendiants, les brigands, les amis de la mort, les arriérés de toutes sortes.—Damnés, si je me vengeais!

Il faut être absolument moderne.

Point de cantiques: tenir le pas gagné. Dure nuit! le sang séché fume sur ma face, et je n'ai rien derrière moi, que cet horrible arbrisseau! . . . Le combat spirituel est aussi brutal que la bataille d'hommes; mais la vision de la justice est le plaisir de Dieu seul.

Cependant c'est la veille. Recevons tous les influx de vigueur et de tendresse réelle. Et, à l'aurore, armé d'une ardente patience, nous entrerons aux splendides villes.

Que parlais-je de main amie! Un bel avantage, c'est que je puis rire de vieilles amours mensongères, et frapper de honte ces couples menteurs,—j'ai vu l'enfer des femmes là-bas;—et il me sera loisible de *posséder la vérité dans une âme et un corps.*

Avril-Août 1873

brigands, of death's friends, of the backward of all kinds. O damned ones, what if I avenged myself!

One must be absolutely modern.

No hymns! Hold the ground gained. Arduous night! The dried blood smokes on my face, and I have nothing behind me but that horrible bush! . . . Spiritual combat is as brutal as the battle of men: but the vision of justice is the pleasure of God alone.

Meanwhile this is the vigil. Welcome then, all the influx of vigor and real tenderness. And, in the dawn, armed with an ardent patience, we shall enter magnificent cities.

Why talk of a friendly hand! My great advantage is that I can laugh at old lying loves and put to shame those deceitful couples,—I saw the hell of women back there;—and I shall be free to *possess truth in one soul and one body*.

April-August 1873

LE BATEAU IVRE

LE BATEAU IVRE

Comme je descendais des Fleuves impassibles,
Je ne me sentis plus guidé par les haleurs:
Des Peaux-Rouges criards les avaient pris pour cibles,
Les ayant cloués nus aux poteaux de couleurs.

J'étais insoucieux de tous les équipages,
Porteur de blés flamands ou de cotons anglais.
Quand avec mes haleurs ont fini ces tapages,
Les Fleuves m'ont laissé descendre où je voulais.

Dans les clapotements furieux des marées,
Moi, l'autre hiver, plus sourd que les cerveaux
d'enfants,
Je courus! Et les Péninsules démarrées
N'ont pas subi tohu-bohus plus triomphants.

THE DRUNKEN BOAT

As I came down the impassible Rivers,
I felt no more the bargemen's guiding hands,
Targets for yelling red-skins they were nailed
Naked to painted poles.

What did I care for any crews,
Carriers of English cotton or of Flemish grain!
Bargemen and all that hubbub left behind,
The waters let me go my own free way.

In the furious lashings of the tides,
Emptier than children's minds, I through that winter
Ran! And great peninsulas unmoored
Never knew more triumphant uproar than I knew.

La tempête a béni mes éveils maritimes.
Plus léger qu'un bouchon j'ai dansé sur les flots
Qu'on appelle rouleurs éternels de victimes,
Dix nuits, sans regretter l'œil niais des falots!

Plus douce qu'aux enfants la chair des pommes sures,
L'eau verte pénétra ma coque de sapin
Et des taches de vins bleus et des vomissures
Me lava, dispersant gouvernail et grappin.

Et dès lors, je me suis baigné dans le Poème
De la Mer, infusé d'astres, et lactescent,
Dévorant les azurs verts; où, flottaison blême
Et ravie, un noyé pensif parfois descend;

Où, teignant tout à coup les bleuités, délires
Et rhythmes lents sous les rutilements du jour,
Plus fortes que l'alcool, plus vastes que nos lyres,
Fermentent les rousseurs amères de l'amour!

Je sais les cieux crevant en éclairs, et les trombes
Et les ressacs et les courants: je sais le soir,
L'Aube exaltée ainsi qu'un peuple de colombes,
Et j'ai vu quelquefois ce que l'homme a cru voir!

THE DRUNKEN BOAT

The tempest blessed my wakings on the sea.
Light as a cork I danced upon the waves,
Eternal rollers of the deep sunk dead,
Nor missed at night the lanterns' idiot eyes!

Sweeter than sour apples to a child,
Green waters seeped through all my seams,
Washing the stains of vomit and blue wine,
And swept away my anchor and my helm.

And since then I've been bathing in the Poem
Of star-infused and milky Sea,
Devouring the azure greens, where, flotsom pale,
A brooding corpse at times drifts by;

Where, dyeing suddenly the blue,
Rhythms delirious and slow in the blaze of day,
Stronger than alcohol, vaster than your lyres,
Ferment the bitter reds of love!

I know the ligntning-opened skies, waterspouts,
Eddies and surfs; I know the night,
And dawn arisen like a colony of doves,
And sometimes I have seen what men have thought
they saw!

J'ai vu le soleil bas, taché d'horreurs mystiques,
Illuminant de longs figements violets,
Pareils à des acteurs de drames très-antiques
Les flots roulant au loin leurs frissons de volets!

J'ai rêvé la nuit verte aux neiges éblouies,
Buser montant aux yeux des mers avec lenteurs,
La circulation des sèves inouïes,
Et l'éveil jaune et bleu des phosphores chanteurs!

J'ai suivi, des mois pleins, pareille aux vacheries
Hystériques, la houle à l'assaut des récifs,
Sans songer que les pieds lumineux des Maries
Pussent forcer le mufle aux Océans poussifs!

J'ai heurté, savez-vous, d'incroyables Florides
Mêlant aux fleurs des yeux de panthères à peaux
D'hommes! Des arcs-en-ciel tendus comme des brides
Sous l'horizon des mers, à de glauques troupeaux!

J'ai vu fermenter les marais énormes, nasses
Où pourrit dans les joncs tout un Léviathan!
Des écroulements d'eaux au milieu des bonaces,
Et les lointains vers les gouffres cataractant!

THE DRUNKEN BOAT

I've seen the low sun, fearful with mystic signs,
Lighting with far flung violet arms,
Like actors in an ancient tragedy,
The fluted waters shivering far away.

I've dreamed green nights of dazzling snows,
Slow kisses on the eyelids of the sea,
The terrible flow of unforgettable saps,
And singing phosphors waking yellow and blue.

Months through I've followed the assaulting tides
Like maddened cattle leaping up the reefs,
Nor ever thought the Marys' luminous feet
Could curb the muzzle of the panting Deep.

I've touched, you know, fantastic Floridas
Mingling the eyes of panthers, human-skinned, with
flowers!
And rainbows stretched like endless reins
To glaucous flocks beneath the seas.

I've seen fermenting marshes like enormous nets
Where in the reeds a whole Leviathan decays!
Crashings of waters in the midst of calms!
Horizons toward far chasms cataracting!

Glaciers, soleils d'argent, flots nacreux, cieux de braises!
Échouages hideux au fond des golfes bruns
Où les serpents géants dévorés des punaises
Choient, des arbres tordus, avec de noirs parfums!

J'aurais voulu montrer aux enfants ces dorades
Du flot bleu, ces poissons d'or, ces poissons chantants.
—Des écumes de fleurs ont bercé mes dérades
Et d'ineffables vents m'ont ailé par instants.

Parfois, martyr lassé des pôles et des zones,
La mer dont le sanglot faisait mon roulis doux
Montait vers moi ses fleurs d'ombre aux ventouses jaunes
Et je restais, ainsi qu'une femme à genoux. . .

Presque île, ballottant sur mes bords les querelles
Et les fientes d'oiseaux clabaudeurs aux yeux blonds.
Et je voguais, lorsqu'à travers mes liens frêles
Des noyés descendaient dormir, à reculons! . . .

Or moi, bateau perdu sous les cheveux des anses,
Jeté par l'ouragan dans l'éther sans oiseau,
Moi dont les Monitors et les voiliers des Hanses
N'auraient pas repêché la carcasse ivre d'eau;

Glaciers and silver suns, fiery skies and pearly seas,
Hideous wrecks at the bottom of brown gulfs
Where giant serpents vermin ridden
Drop with black perfumes from the twisted trees!

I would show children those dorados,
And golden singing fishes in blue seas.
Foam flowers have blest my aimless wanderings,
Ineffable winds have given me wings.

Tired of poles and zones, sometimes the martyred sea,
Rolling me gently on her sobbing breast,
Lifted her shadow flowers with yellow cups toward me
And I stayed there like a woman on her knees.

Island, I sailed, and on my gunnels tossed
Quarrels and droppings of the pale-eyed birds,
While floating slowly past my fragile bands,
Backward the drowned went dreaming by.

But I, lost boat in the cove's trailing tresses,
Tossed by the tempest into birdless space,
Whose water-drunken carcass never would have sal-
valged
Old Monitor or Galleon of the Hanseatic League;

Libre, fumant, monté de brumes violettes,
Moi qui trouais le ciel rougeoyant comme un mur
Qui porte, confiture exquise aux bons poëtes,
Des lichens de soleil et des morves d'azur;

Qui courais, taché de lunules électriques,
Planche folle, escorté des hippocampes noirs,
Quand les juillets faisaient crouler à coups de triques
Les cieux ultramarins aux ardents entonnoirs;

Moi qui tremblais, sentant geindre à cinquante lieues
Le rut des Béhémots et les Maelstroms épais,
Fileur éternel des immobilités bleues,
Je regrette l'Europe aux anciens parapets!

J'ai vu des archipels sidéraux! et des îles
Dont les cieux délirants sont ouverts au vogueur:
—Est-ce en ces nuits sans fonds que tu dors et t'exiles,
Million d'oiseaux d'or, ô future Vigueur?—

Mais, vrai, j'ai trop pleuré! Les Aubes sont navrantes.
Toute lune est atroce et tout soleil amer:
L'âcre amour m'a gonflé de torpeurs enivrantes.
O que ma quille éclate! O que j'aille à la mer!

Who, ridden by violet mists, steaming and free,
Pierced the sky reddening like a wall,
Covered with lichens of the sun and azure's phlem,
Preserves that all good poets love,

Who, spotted with electric crescents ran,
Mad plank with escort of black hypocamps,
While Augusts with their hammer blows tore down
The sea-blue, spiral-flaming skies;

Who trembling felt Behemoth's rut
And Maelstroms groaning fifty leagues away,
Eternal scudder through the quiescent blue,
I long for Europe's parapets!

I've seen sidereal archipelagos! Islands
Whose delirious skies open for wanderers:
"Is it in such bottomless nights you sleep, exiled,
O countless golden birds, O Force to come?"

True I have wept too much! Dawns are heartbreaking;
Cruel all moons and bitter the suns.
Drunk with love's acrid torpors,
O let my keel burst! Let me go to the sea!

Si je désire une eau d'Europe, c'est la flache
Noire et froide où vers le crépuscule embaumé
Un enfant accroupi plein de tristesses, lâche
Un bateau frêle comme un papillon de mai.

Je ne puis plus, baigné de vos langueurs, ô lames,
Enlever leur sillage aux porteurs de cotons,
Ni traverser l'orgueil des drapeaux et des flammes,
Ni nager sous les yeux horribles des pontons.

If I desire any European water, it's the black pond
And cold, where toward perfumed evening
A sad child on his knees sets sail
A boat as frail as a May butterfly.

I can no longer, bathed in your languors, O waves,
Obliterate the cotton carriers' wake,
Nor cross the pride of pennants and of flags,
Nor swim past prison hulks' hateful eyes!

New Directions Paperbooks—A Partial Listing

Walter Abish, *How German Is It*. NDP508.
Ahmed Ali, *Twilight in Delhi*. NDP782.
John Allman, *Scenarios for a Mixed Landscape*. NDP619.
Alfred Andersch, *Efraim's Book*. NDP779.
Sherwood Anderson, *Poor White*. NDP763.
Wayne Andrews, *The Surrealist Parade*. NDP689.
David Antin, *Tuning*. NDP570.
G. Apollinaire, *Selected Writings*.† NDP310.
Jimmy S. Baca, *Martín & Meditations*. NDP648.
Djuna Barnes, *Nightwood*. NDP98.
J. Barzun, *An Essay on French Verse*. NDP708
H. E. Bates, *A Month by the Lake*. NDP669.
A Party for the Girls. NDP653.
Charles Baudelaire, *Flowers of Evil*. †NDP684.
Paris Spleen. NDP294.
Bei Dao, *Old Snow*. NDP727.
Gottfried Benn, *Primal Vision*. NDP322.
Adolfo Bioy Casares, *A Russian Doll*. NDP745.
Carmel Bird, *The Bluebird Café*. NDP707.
Johannes Bobrowski, *Shadow Lands*. NDP788.
Wolfgang Borchert, *The Man Outside*. NDP319.
Jorge Luis Borges, *Labyrinths*. NDP186.
Seven Nights. NDP576.
Kay Boyle, *The Crazy Hunter*. NDP770.
Fifty Stories. NDP741.
Kamau Brathwaite, *MiddlePassages*. NDP776.
Black + Blues. NDP815.
William Bronk, *Selected Poems*. NDP816.
M. Bulgakov, *Flight & Bliss*. NDP593.
The Life of M. de Moliere. NDP601.
Frederick Busch, *Absent Friends*. NDP721.
Veza Canetti, *Yellow Street*. NDP709.
Ernesto Cardenal, *Zero Hour*. NDP502.
Anne Carson, *Glass, Irony & God*. NDP808.
Joyce Cary, *Mister Johnson*. NDP631.
Hayden Carruth, *Tell Me Again. . . .* NDP677.
Camilo José Cela, *Mazurka for Two Dead Men*. NDP789.
Louis-Ferdinand Céline,
Death on the Installment Plan. NDP330.
Journey to the End of the Night. NDP542.
René Char. *Selected Poems*. †NDP734.
Jean Cocteau, *The Holy Terrors*. NDP212.
M. Collis, *She Was a Queen*. NDP716.
Gregory Corso, *Long Live Man*. NDP127.
Herald of the Autochthonic Spirit. NDP522.
Robert Creeley, *Windows*. NDP687.
Guy Davenport, *7 Greeks*. NDP799.
Margaret Dawe, *Nissequott*. NDP775.
Osamu Dazai, *The Setting Sun*. NDP258.
No Longer Human. NDP357.
Mme. de Lafayette, *The Princess of Cleves*. NDP660.
E. Dujardin, *We'll to the Woods No More*. NDP682.
Robert Duncan, *Selected Poems*. NDP754.
Wm. Empson, *7 Types of Ambiguity*. NDP204
Some Versions of Pastoral. NDP92.
S. Endo, *The Sea and the Poison*. NDP737.
Caradoc Evans, *Nothing to Pay*. NDP800.
Wm. Everson, *The Residual Years*. NDP263.
Lawrence Ferlinghetti, *A Coney Island of the Mind*. NDP74.
These Are My Rivers. NDP786.
Ronald Firbank, *Five Novels*. NDP581.
Three More Novels. NDP614.
F. Scott Fitzgerald, *The Crack-up*. NDP757.
Gustave Flaubert, *Dictionary*. NDP230.
J. Gahagan, *Did Gustav Mahler Ski?* NDP711.
Gandhi, *Gandhi on Non-Violence*. NDP197.
Gary, Romain, *Promise at Dawn*. NDP635.
W. Gerhardie, *Futility*. NDP722.
Goethe, *Faust*, Part I. NDP70.
Allen Grossman, *Philosopher's Window*. NDP807.
Martin Grzimek, *Shadowlife*. NDP705.
Guigonnat, Henri, *Daemon in Lithuania*. NDP592.
Lars Gustafsson, *The Death of a Beekeeper*. NDP523.
A Tiler's Afternoon. NDP761.
John Hawkes, *The Beetle Leg*. NDP239.
Second Skin. NDP146.
Samuel Hazo, *To Paris*. NDP512.
H. D. *Collected Poems*. NDP611.
Helen in Egypt. NDP380.
HERmione. NDP526.
Selected Poems. NDP658.
Tribute to Freud. NDP572.
Herman Hesse, *Siddhartha*. NDP65.
Susan Howe, *The Nonconformist's Memorial*. NDP755.
Vicente Huidobro, *Selected Poetry*. NDP520.
C. Isherwood, *All the Conspirators*. NDP480.
The Berlin Stories. NDP134.
Lêdo Ivo, *Snake's Nest*. NDP521.
Fleur Jaeggy, *Sweet Days of Discipline*. NDP758.
Henry James, *The Sacred Fount*. NDP790.
Gustav Janouch. *Conversations with Kafka*. NDP313.
Alfred Jarry, *Ubu Roi*. NDP105.
Robinson Jeffers, *Cawdor and Medea*. NDP293.
B. S. Johnson, *Christie Malry's. . . .* NDP600.
G. Josipovici, *In a Hotel Garden*. NDP801.
James Joyce, *Stephen Hero*. NDP133.
Franz Kafka, *Amerika*. NDP117.
Mary Karr, *The Devil's Tour*. NDP768.
Bob Kaufman, *The Ancient Rain*. NDP514.
John Keene, *Annotations*. NDP809.
H. von Kleist, *Prince Friedrich*. NDP462.
Dezsö Kosztolányi, *Anna Édes*. NDP772.
Rüdiger Kremer, *The Color of Snow*. NDP743.
M. Krleža, *On the Edge of Reason*. NDP810.
Jules Laforgue, *Moral Tales*. NDP594.
P. Lal, *Great Sanskrit Plays*. NDP142.
Tommaso Landolfi, *Gogol's Wife*. NDP155.
D. Larsen, *Stitching Porcelain*. NDP710.
James Laughlin, *Remembering W. C. Williams*. NDP811.
Lautréamont, *Maldoror*. NDP207.
Siegfried Lenz, *The German Lesson*. NDP618.
Denise Levertov, *Breathing the Water*. NDP640.
Collected Earlier Poems 1940–60 NDP475.
A Door in the Hive. NDP685.
Evening Train. NDP750.
New & Selected Essays. NDP749.
Poems 1960–1967. NDP549.
Poems 1968–1972. NDP629.
Harry Levin, *James Joyce*. NDP87.
Li Ch'ing-chao, *Complete Poems*. NDP492.
Enrique Lihn, *The Dark Room*. †NDP542.
C. Lispector, *Soulstorm*. NDP671.
The Hour of the Star. NDP733.
Garciá Lorca, *Five Plays*. NDP232.
The Public & Play Without a Title. NDP561.
Selected Poems. †NDP114.
Three Tragedies. NDP52.
Francisco G. Lorca, *In The Green Morning*. NDP610.
Michael McClure, *Simple Eyes*. NDP780.
Carson McCullers, *The Member of the Wedding*. (Playscript) NDP153.
X. de Maistre, *Voyage Around My Room*. NDP791.
Stéphane Mallarme,† *Selected Poetry and Prose*. NDP529.
Bernadette Mayer, *A Bernadette Mayer Reader*. NDP739.
Thomas Merton, *Asian Journal*. NDP394.
New Seeds of Contemplation. NDP337.
Selected Poems. NDP85.
Thoughts on the East. NDP802.
The Way of Chuang Tzu. NDP276.
Zen and the Birds of Appetite. NDP261.
Henri Michaux, *A Barbarian in Asia*. NDP622.
Selected Writings. NDP264.
Henry Miller, *The Air-Conditioned Nightmare*. NDP302.
Aller Retour New York. NDP753.
Big Sur & The Oranges. NDP161.

†Bilingual

The Colossus of Maroussi. NDP75.
A Devil in Paradise. NDP765.
Into the Heart of Life. NDP728.
The Smile at the Foot of the Ladder. NDP386.
Y. Mishima, *Confessions of a Mask*. NDP253.
Death in Midsummer. NDP215.
Frédéric Mistral, *The Memoirs*. NDP632.
Eugenio Montale, *It Depends*.† NDP507.
Selected Poems.† NDP193.
Paul Morand, *Fancy Goods/Open All Night*. NDP567.
Vladimir Nabokov, *Nikolai Gogol*. NDP78.
Laughter in the Dark. NDP729.
The Real Life of Sebastian Knight. NDP432.
P. Neruda, *The Captain's Verses*.† NDP345.
Residence on Earth.† NDP340.
Fully Empowered. NDP792.
New Directions in Prose & Poetry (Anthology).
Available from #17 forward to #55.
Robert Nichols, *Arrival*. NDP437.
J. F. Nims, *The Six-Cornered Snowflake*. NDP700.
Charles Olson, *Selected Writings*. NDP231.
Toby Olson, *The Life of Jesus*. NDP417.
George Oppen, *Collected Poems*. NDP418.
István Örkeny, *The Flower Show/*
The Toth Family. NDP536.
Wilfred Owen, *Collected Poems*. NDP210.
José Emilio Pacheco, *Battles in the Desert*. NDP637.
Selected Poems.† NDP638.
Michael Palmer, *At Passages*. NDP803.
Nicanor Parra, *Antipoems: New & Selected*. NDP603.
Boris Pasternak, *Safe Conduct*. NDP77.
Kenneth Patchen, *Because It Is*. NDP83.
Collected Poems. NDP284.
Selected Poems. NDP160.
Ota Pavel, *How I Came to Know Fish*. NDP713.
Octavio Paz, *Collected Poems*. NDP719.
Configurations.† NDP303.
—*A Draft of Shadows*.† NDP489.
Selected Poems. NDP574.
Sunstone.† NDP735.
A Tree Within.† NDP661.
St. John Perse, *Selected Poems*.† NDP545.
Ezra Pound, *ABC of Reading*. NDP89.
Confucius. NDP285.
Confucius to Cummings. (Anth.) NDP126.
Diptych Rome-London. NDP783.
A Draft of XXX Cantos. NDP690.
Elektra. NDP683.
Guide to Kulchur. NDP257.
Literary Essays. NDP250.
Personae. NDP697.
Selected Cantos. NDP304.
Selected Poems. NDP66.
The Spirit of Romance. NDP266.
Eça de Queiroz, *Illustrious House of Ramires*. NDP785.
Raymond Queneau, *The Blue Flowers*. NDP595.
Exercises in Style. NDP513.
Mary de Rachewiltz, *Ezra Pound*. NDP405.
Raja Rao, *Kanthapura*. NDP224.
Herbert Read, *The Green Child*. NDP208.
P. Reverdy, *Selected Poems*.† NDP346.
Kenneth Rexroth, *An Autobiographical Novel*. NDP725.
Classics Revisited. NDP621.
More Classics Revisited. NDP668.
Flower Wreath Hill. NDP724.
100 Poems from the Chinese. NDP192.
100 Poems from the Japanese.† NDP147.
Selected Poems. NDP581.
Women Poets of China. NDP528.
Women Poets of Japan. NDP527.
Rainer Maria Rilke, *Poems from*
The Book of Hours. NDP408.
Possibility of Being. (Poems). NDP436.
Where Silence Reigns. (Prose). NDP464.
Arthur Rimbaud. *Illuminations*.† NDP56.
Season in Hell & Drunken Boat.† NDP97.
Edouard Roditi, *Delights of Turkey*. NDP445.
Jerome Rothenberg, *Khurbn*. NDP679.
The Lorca Variations. NDP771.
Nayantara Sahgal, *Rich Like Us*. NDP665.
Ihara Saikaku, *The Life of an Amorous Woman*.
NDP270.
St. John of the Cross, *Poems*.† NDP341.
William Saroyan, *Fresno Stories*. NDP793.
Jean-Paul Sartre, *Nausea*. NDP82.
The Wall (*Intimacy*). NDP272.
P. D. Scott, *Crossing Borders*. NDP796.
Listening to the Candle. NDP747.
Delmore Schwartz, *Selected Poems*. NDP241.
In Dreams Begin Responsibilities. NDP454.
Hasan Shah, *The Dancing Girl*. NDP777.
K. Shiraishi, *Seasons of Sacred Lust*. NDP453.
Stevie Smith, *Collected Poems*. NDP562.
Novel on Yellow Paper. NDP778.
A Very Pleasant Evening. NDP804.
Gary Snyder, *The Back Country*. NDP249.
Turtle Island. NDP381.
Gustaf Sobin, *Breaths' Burials*. NDP781.
Muriel Spark, *The Comforters*. NDP796.
The Driver's Seat. NDP786.
The Public Image. NDP767.
Enid Starkie, *Rimbaud*. NDP254.
Stendhal, *Three Italian Chronicles*. NDP704.
Antonio Tabucchi, *Indian Nocturne*. NDP666.
Nathaniel Tarn, *Lyrics . . . Bride of God*. NDP391.
Dylan Thomas, *Adventures in Skin Trade*. NDP183.
A Child's Christmas in Wales. NDP812.
Collected Poems 1934–1952. NDP316.
Collected Stories. NDP626.
Portrait of the Artist as a Young Dog. NDP51.
Quite Early One Morning. NDP90.
Under Milk Wood. NDP73.
Tian Wen: A Chinese Book of Origins. NDP624.
Uwe Timm, *The Snake Tree*. NDP686.
Lionel Trilling, *E. M. Forster*. NDP189.
Tu Fu, *Selected Poems*. NDP675.
N. Tucci, *The Rain Came Last*. NDP688.
Paul Valéry, *Selected Writings*.† NDP184.
Elio Vittorini, *A Vittorini Omnibus*. NDP366.
Rosmarie Waldrop, *A Key into the Language of America*.
NDP798.
Robert Penn Warren, *At Heaven's Gate*. NDP588.
Eliot Weinberger, *Outside Stories*. NDP751.
Nathanael West, *Miss Lonelyhearts &*
Day of the Locust. NDP125.
J. Wheelwright, *Collected Poems*. NDP544.
Tennessee Williams, *Baby Doll*. NDP714.
Cat on a Hot Tin Roof. NDP398.
Collected Stories. NDP784.
The Glass Menagerie. NDP218.
Hard Candy. NDP225.
A Lovely Sunday for Creve Coeur. NDP497.
Red Devil Battery Sign. NDP650.
The Roman Spring of Mrs. Stone. NDP770.
A Streetcar Named Desire. NDP501.
Sweet Bird of Youth. NDP409.
Twenty-Seven Wagons Full of Cotton. NDP217.
Vieux Carre. NDP482.
William Carlos Williams. *Asphodel*. NDP794.
The Autobiography. NDP223.
Collected Poems: Vol. I. NDP730.
Collected Poems: Vol. II. NDP731.
The Doctor Stories. NDP585.
Imaginations. NDP329.
In The American Grain. NDP53.
In The Money. NDP240.
Paterson. NDP806.
Pictures from Brueghel. NDP118.
Selected Poems (new ed.). NDP602.
White Mule. NDP226.
Wisdom Books:
St. Francis. NDP477; *Taoists*. NDP509;
Wisdom of the Desert. NDP295; *Zen Masters*.
NDP415.

†Bilingual